Breaking Free

MAKING THE IMPOSSIBLE CHRISTIAN LIFE POSSIBLE

Hannah Morrell

KW
Kingdom Winds
PUBLISHING

Copyright © 2024 by Hannah Morrell.

All rights reserved. No part of this publication may be reproduced, distributed, or transmitted in any form or by any means, including photocopying, recording, or other electronic or mechanical methods, without the prior written permission of the publisher, except in the case of brief quotations embodied in critical reviews and certain other noncommercial uses permitted by copyright law. For permission requests, write to the publisher at publishing@kingdomwinds.com.

All Scripture quotations are from The Passion Translation®. Copyright © 2017, 2018, 2020 by Passion & Fire Ministries, Inc. Used by permission. All rights reserved. ThePassionTranslation.com.

First Edition, 2024.

ISBN 13: 978-1-64590-060-3

Published by Kingdom Winds Publishing.

www.kingdomwinds.com

publishing@kingdomwinds.com

Printed in the United States of America.

The views expressed in this book are not necessarily those of the publisher.

Table of Contents

Introduction	5
Salvation	11
Abiding	31
Your Past & Flesh Pattern	47
How Do We Abide?	65
Who Is God?	79
What Does God Want From Us?	95
What Do We Do With People?	109
What Do I Do With Myself?	127
What Do We Do With Suffering?	141
How Do We Live With Hope in Our Present?	157
Recommended Reading	173

Hannah Morrell

For Mike Wells,

who never failed to encourage,
challenge, and love me into a deeper
relationship with our amazing Jesus.

Introduction

You may think that living the Christian life is extremely boring or nearly impossible. Waves of guilt and shame combine with a constant feeling of inadequacy to create a life of judgement and self-condemnation. At every turn, you encounter another reason that you don't measure up or need to be doing more. You obsess over what you see as your failures and think that this mental self-mutilation will somehow make a difference next time. Your heart lays bleeding and torn after you've beaten yourself with all the messages you have received throughout life from those who have done you wrong. Comparison and self-righteousness have provided no relief, and you just want something real. Yuck!

I hope, in the pages to come, to show you the contrast of this outlook with the life I believe Jesus intended us to live when He died for us in the first place: a life of joy and overflowing love that fills us up with acceptance and belonging. That acceptance and belonging then spill over to those around us as mercy and grace pouring out over every step.

The Christian life doesn't require us to do more or be more; rather, it provides an exchange of our junk for God's perfection, strength, and peace that allows us to live completely differently. This life is about rest, not more striving. It is about love and belonging, not more rejection. It is about being able to live in the impossible while accessing the strength of the God of the universe to move forward. It is about living in the faith of Jesus, rather than condemning ourselves for not being able to drum up enough faith on our own.

God created us for relationship, first with Himself and then with other people. But these relationships often bring trouble as pain and discouragement result from their messiness. Relationship, in its proper place, provides the foundation for living. The order must be right, though, for us to enjoy it. Relationship with God is the basis for love, acceptance, rest, peace, joy, and everything else we need to live. Relationship with humans can be wonderful, but it must follow a relationship with God in order for us not to be mangled and torn up by the crazy humans we encounter through life.

I want to take you on a journey of transforming your life through the abiding life—the life of step-by-step, moment-by-moment connection with God, which becomes the most practical basis in the world for everything else. This abiding life transforms every day into one of beauty, sweet closeness, and peace that makes no sense given the circumstances. It allows us to rise above any situation, seeing past it because our position has never been one of being drowned by problems. We are seated with Christ in the heavenlies (Ephesians 2:6), and we can embrace all of life from that position as we allow God to change our perspective. This shift doesn't keep away the pain, but it does take our pain from something soul-crushing or life-ending to something we can use as a steppingstone to launch us forward. We can experience comfort and tenderness in the pain rather than constant rejection, depression, and anxiety.

This may sound far-fetched—like a fantasy. You may want to bring me back down to earth and tell me to live more realistically. But I would argue that living in relationship with the One who made me, knows me inside and out, and knows exactly what I need is the most realistic life possible. If I can live free from all the pressures of the world, rising above political situations, corruption, financial pressures and woes, I think the abiding life—living in relationship with God rather than living by a set of religious rules- becomes more practical and life-giving than any other way of doing life.

Even if you remain unconvinced, tiptoe along this path with me as I introduce you to the life God created you to live, thriving rather than surviving, a life in which you are not just living for the great someday but can experience heaven and eternal life right now.

My prayer for you is that you will experience the transformation of the abiding life and never want to go back to the old way again. No one is ever too broken, too exhausted, or too much of anything to experience this life as God intended us to live it.

So, don't hold back—let's dive in to explore this life together and see what we get to leave behind and what we get to push towards. Don't you need a break, a rest from the pressures and cares of life? Let's venture onward toward rest.

Breaking Free

Hannah Morrell

Salvation

Jesus does not divide the world into the moral "good guys" and the immoral "bad guys". He shows us that everyone is dedicated to a project of self-salvation, to using God and others in order to get power and control for themselves. We are just going about it in different ways. Even though both sons [in the parable of the prodigal son] are wrong, however, the father cares for them and invites them both back into his love and feast.

—Tim Keller[1]

I love watching artists create beautiful things.

- A chef with a masterpiece of flavor, texture, and color, plating a dish with care after hours of preparation.
- A painter with only a brush and a few pots of paint, bringing a world of imagination to life with a thought and a few pencil strokes.
- A sculptor who, like Michelangelo, sees a sculpture already complete within a formation of the hardest type of rock painstakingly etching away to release his vision to be free and admired by the world.

---

1 Keller, Timothy. *The Prodigal God: Recovering the Heart of the Christian Faith.* New York: Penguin Books, 2008.

❀ A musician who captures an emotion within an instrument's range of notes, taking us on a journey of discovery into the beauty of sound.

God, the Trinity of the Father, the Son, and the Holy Spirit, has always loved us. We see that love in the gentleness of His creation: He speaks, puts to sleep, and forms (Genesis 1). These are statements of tenderness and of an artist bringing forth a masterpiece from His chosen medium. God's word does not return void (Isaiah 55:11). It speaks life into being.

God created Adam and Eve, the first people, in His own image (Genesis 1:27). They were His image-bearers. They were not God, but they were like God. The poisonous lie of the enemy through the serpent was that they could BECOME like God if they ate the fruit of the tree God had commanded them not to eat (Genesis 2:5). But they already <u>WERE</u> LIKE God! The enemy is constantly trying to get us to work for something we already have. This is distracting and unproductive. But sadly, we buy into the lie and run with it.

God knew Adam and Eve were going to blow it, and really, He knew we would, too. Each of us wants to blame the first people for being duped, but I believe each of us would choose the same way. The desire within us is to become our own god, and we dismiss God's gift of love in order to achieve it.

I love the theme of the *Jesus Storybook Bible*— God's never stopping, never giving up, unbreaking, always and forever love—all the way through.[2]

---

[2] Lloyd-Jones, Sally. *Jesus Storybook Bible: Every Story Whispers His Name*. Michigan: Zonderkids, 2007.

Breaking Free

Too often, we assume the Old Testament God was an obnoxious jerk and that Jesus pacified the New Testament God. That is not the story of the Old Testament. God was highly involved in the lives of His people all the way through, reaching for them in relationship in whatever capacity they could see Him. Many experienced this relationship with Him—Abraham, Sarah, Isaac, Jacob, Moses, Gideon, and Deborah, to name a few. God put a sacrificial system in place, but really, He desired connection with His people rather than the sacrifice of sheep and bulls (Hosea 6:6).

The intention of the law was to create a pathway to relationship. Don't eat the fruit of this tree so we can walk together, and you won't be afraid (Genesis 2:17). Don't worship idols and have unholy things in your camp so I, in my holiness, can live with you in the heart of the tabernacle (Exodus 20:4–5). I will be with you and make my presence visual through a cloud during the day and a column of fire at night (Exodus 13:21–22). I will show up through miracles, rescuing you over and over from your own prideful self-reliance. Those are the barriers to relationship, and God wanted to reach across those even as people erected more.

Unfortunately, humanity seeks something to worship and give attention to that helps them to have some sense of control or direction. This leads us to a place of creating more rules and limiting our access to relationship based on these rules. The word "religion" comes from the Latin word *relegere*, which means "to bind again," and this binding up leads us to worship the rules rather than the God who has been, from the beginning, trying to have relationship with us. [3] God is calling us to an abiding life that allows us to be free from religious binding to walk in a living, breathing relationship, worshipping Him rather than a system of rules. Living as a branch on the Vine (John 15) was never about following rules or earning God's approval by doing life perfectly. Instead, the abiding life gives us freedom to be in dependence and real relationship with the God who attaches us to the Vine and keeps us grafted in and producing fruit through His empowerment.

God was loving in the Old Testament. He loved enough to bring to life a creation He knew would reject Him. But He had a plan to sacrifice Himself to make a way for that creation to be with Him. This way required nothing of His people but acceptance. Consider that for a moment if you don't believe God loves you.

The Path to Relationship

> Jesus explained, "I am the Way, I am the Truth, and I am the Life. No one comes next to the Father except through union with me. To know me is to know my Father too. And from now on you will realize that you have seen him and experienced him."
> John 14:6–7

Jesus came to be the Way. He is the way to relationship with the Trinity—the Father, Son, and Holy Spirit. We needed a Way because our way wasn't (and maybe isn't) working.

I tend to be a bit stubborn about my way. When I think I know a method to fix something or the best way to do whatever

---

[3] "Religion." *Merriam-Webster.com Dictionary*, Merriam-Webster, https://www.merriam-webster.com/dictionary/religion. Accessed 11 Mar. 2024.

Breaking Free

is in front of me, I really have to come crashing into a brick wall before I will turn and admit that perhaps I don't have the best plan to move ahead. I have tried to be good, to avoid wrong, and to measure up to whatever standard I believed God and everyone else had for me.

My way basically just wore me out. I was exhausted and unsuccessful because I never could quite meet the standard I believed was being used to judge me at every step. I kept needing a bigger or greater sacrifice to scale the mountain I believed was between God and me. One day, a friend told me that my standard was higher than God's. I couldn't even comprehend what that meant because I had created a god in my mind who was so critical and condemning. How could this be?

I believe this kind of perspective may be why so many Christians become burned out and frustrated by trying to live the Christian life. When we believe it's up to us to perform well enough to gain God's love and acceptance, we tire quickly and realize it is futility. We might even become angry that this is the supposed expectation. Because we can't meet it.

Those who are trying to obey all the rules, who put God in a place where He must give us a gold star for our performances, become "religious." These people (and I've been one of them) live in constant fear. They are afraid of tarnished reputations, of seeming inadequate, and of not being honored as the incredible person they are trying to be. Some are deeply insecure because they see the truth beneath the failings and mistakes they keep trying to cover up or ignore, hoping that no one else will notice them. Some are incredibly arrogant because of the hard work they have done to convince themselves and everyone else that they have achieved the standard.

I think of 1 Corinthians 13 when I observe religious people or those who weaponize God's word to attack and destroy. Some, such as during the Crusades, physically transformed sections or verses of the written Word of God, making them into weapons that they wielded to "evangelize" those who did not agree. Others use manipulation and judgement to threaten others into trying to maintain the façade. 1 Corinthians 13 quickly derails this tactic.

> If I were to speak with eloquence in earth's many languages, and in the heavenly tongues of angels, yet I didn't express myself with love, my words would be reduced to the hollow sound of nothing more than a clanging cymbal. And if I were to have the gift of prophecy with a profound understanding of God's hidden secrets, and if I possessed unending supernatural knowledge, and if I had the greatest gift of faith that could move mountains, but have never learned to love, then I am nothing. And if I were to be so generous as to give away everything I owned to feed the poor, and to offer my body to be burned as a martyr, without the pure motive of love, I would gain nothing of value.
> 1 Corinthians 13:1–3

Without love, we have created a religion void of relationship. An old friend told me that the Christian religion was one of the most poisonous of religions because it took the gift of Jesus' sacrifice and love and turned it into how we should try to earn His approval.

My friend is right: religion has lost sight of relationship in striving to embody an ideal. But this isn't what Christian faith, relationship with God, looks like. Christian faith isn't about being incredibly moral; it's about being incredibly loved. We needed a path to relationship that did not depend on our doing right or avoiding wrong, but rather dependent on God's doing, His reaching out to us. This abiding life, or living in relationship, changes everything as we acknowledge God has already given us everything we need for pleasing Him in Christ.

> CHRISTIAN FAITH ISN'T ABOUT BEING INCREDIBLY MORAL; IT'S ABOUT BEING INCREDIBLY LOVED.

The Sacrifice for Relationship

For the greatest love of all is a love that sacrifices all. And this great love is demonstrated when a person sacrifices his life for his friends.
John 15:13

The stories and movies I like the best are those which illustrate the love of one person for another, often at great cost and sacrifice. *Braveheart, Hunger Games, The Last of the Mohicans*: each of these stories is built around the theme of someone offering himself to save another.

Because we are sinners and cannot have relationship with God on our own, Christ laid down His life for the love of us (Romans 5:8–9). Jesus volunteered to come die and rise again so that we could have the life He had always intended for us—the life lived in relationship with God. If you ever doubt your worth, remember how much worth Jesus bestowed on your life.

Jesus willingly suffered rejection, physical torture, emotional betrayal, abandonment, and walking through death itself to free us from our sin, the result of our trying to be like God. The lie that we needed something we didn't have yet and would find it in any number of places outside of God started in the Garden with Adam and Eve. Sinful decisions to make our own way without God imprison us, and we needed a way out that we couldn't provide for ourselves. He endured all this awfulness, not to present us with a list of rules to follow, but so that He can walk with us and live life with us.

I think we often look at Jesus' death and resurrection as the most difficult sacrifice He made, but I wonder sometimes if living with us every day isn't an almost equal sacrifice! He made Himself available for all of this, bringing resurrection life to every dead part of us.

We can never earn or deserve this sacrifice (Ephesians 2:8). In fact, Jesus died for us while we hated Him, while we were His enemies (Romans 5:8–9). He didn't wait until we had finally gotten close enough to bridge the gap. We were just a massive mess, proving over and over that we could not make our way to Him, so while we were far away, He brought us near and made a way to take us back with Him (Ephesians 2:13).

So, instead of waiting until we feel we have earned or deserve His love, we must simply receive. To receive, we need to put down pride and unbelief, embracing humility and faith. I watched a show one time where a man was adamant that he didn't want to pray in the middle of a scary situation. When pressed for a reason, he finally admitted he just didn't want help. He wanted to look back and see that he had done it for himself by himself. Pride says, "life is all up to me," and unbelief says, "God isn't doing a darn thing about it."

Breaking Free

Humility and faith are counter-cultural in the United States. This culture says that to be a success, one must be a self-made man or woman. Society doesn't tolerate or accept weakness, so one must pull oneself up by the bootstraps and push to succeed.

One day, I was at the park while my kids were playing. I watched a little boy, maybe 4 years old, try to kiss his father on the cheek before he ran off to play. The man pulled away as if struck, to avoid his son's affection. Why? My guess would be that he couldn't move in humility for the love of his boy. He had to maintain a tough-guy image, and that didn't jive with a kiss on the cheek from his son.

We must set aside our images of toughness, independence, and self-reliance. They are not serving us; instead, they are driving a wedge in our relationships with God or other people. While society demands independence and self-reliance, God asks for dependence and God-reliance. We can learn to celebrate our weaknesses, because our weakness reveals Jesus's strength (2 Corinthians 12:9–11); we become a portal for His strength when we admit and walk in weakness. Dependence is the way we honor Jesus' sacrifice for us.

What Happens in Acceptance?

> Now, if anyone is enfolded into Christ, he has become an entirely new person. All that is related to the old order has vanished. Behold, everything is fresh and new.
>
> 2 Corinthians 5:17

What happens when we accept Jesus's sacrifice and new life? We become new creations! When we receive the life of Christ, given for us, we are no longer orphans but have become legitimate daughters or sons of the amazing God of the universe (Galatians 4:7). We are enfolded in Him, and He is in us (John 17:23). He has transferred us from the kingdom of darkness to the kingdom of light (Colossians 1:13–14). We can live as a branch on the Vine as God intended, in dependence and abiding life with the life of the Vine flowing through us (John 15). We can live differently as we are no longer under the burden of sin, and are free to live in relationship with God as we were meant to do.

I have a couple of friends who live in Haiti. They are both single gals who moved to that country more than 15 years ago to work with an orphanage that helped kids become adopted by families in the United States and Canada. While working with this orphanage, the Haitian government shut down another "orphanage" that was discovered to be a festering hell of abuse, child prostitution, and starvation. The kids who had been confined in this institution had been so wounded and broken that they were deemed "unadoptable" to other countries, so extended family members in Haiti were sought for placement options.

Breaking Free

After most of the kids had been placed, ten kids remained with no discoverable extended family. No place could be found for them. Following their rescue from the abusive facility, the ten entered my friends' orphanage, where they watched as babies and other children arrived and were adopted out to families. They watched for three years, never able to be adopted themselves or to find a settled home. During this time, God called my friend Joyce to adopt all ten children. She did not know what that meant or exactly how it all would work, but she knew clearly that God was calling her to this.

Joyce left the orphanage where she worked, established a nonprofit ministry to support the new endeavor, located a house with space to contain a large family, and adopted all ten of the kids who had been deemed "unadoptable" and who were without future or hope. God called her heart to see beyond the painful past and the present brokenness of these kids to see who they really were. She saw who God saw them to be. Melissa, my other friend, had adopted a Haitian girl and began helping to support the household by contributing much to the kids and to their raising. These kids who had been told they could never belong now have a place they call home. They have a new last name. The ladies are working to acquire birth certificates for the kids, as they had all previously been without documentation. They are being told and shown that they have worth, and they are safe. They have a family who loves them.

This is exactly what God has done for us. He has taken us, the "unadoptable" mess that we were, and received us with great joy into His house, telling us that now we belong, that we matter, and that He loves us. He has changed our name from outcast to beloved, bestowing relationship on us that we never could have deserved. We are still messy, but we are His! We have access to all the resources of our Dad's house and can live in an entirely different way in accepting Him as our true Father.

What Are We Saved For?

> For it was always in his perfect plan to adopt us as his delightful children, through our union with Jesus, the Anointed One, so that his tremendous love that cascades over us would glorify his grace—for the same love he has for the Beloved, Jesus, he has for us. And this unfolding plan brings him great pleasure!
> Ephesians 1:5–6

When we look at this salvation, at this adoption, we often consider what Jesus has saved us FROM, but we overlook what He saved us FOR! God created us to be in relationship with Himself, Father, Son, and Spirit. This relationship is a return to our original design! It's normal life, what God intended for us the whole time as we get to enjoy the abiding life with Him. Life was actually meant to be full of joy and freedom.

> IN THIS NEW LIFE, COMMANDMENTS BECOME PROMISES.

In this new life, commandments become promises. We no longer see a list condemning and judging us into failure. Instead, what is true about Christ has become true about us. This isn't dependent on our strength or determination (thank goodness!) but an acceptance, again, of what is now true about us. This means that with Jesus, we recognize the things to which God has said "no" are not good for us and will bring harm. And, we recognize the things to which God says "yes" are possible only because of God's strength within—which we have!

As you read the Bible, what if you considered it in these terms? I cannot love my enemy, but because of God's love, love is promised through me! Not by my rationalizing or trying to make sense of a situation—but by my admission of weakness and turning to the One who is my strength. I cannot be patient, but He is patient through me! No more condemnation for us (Romans 8:1); now, we can have the power to live out anything that God asks because He is providing His power for us to do so.

Another gift we receive is that our failures no longer define us! As my friend, Mike Wells, used to say, "When we fall, we fall into God." So often when we talk about our lives, we try to only hit the highlights while secretly obsessing over the failures. We live in regret, which is so poisonous to our minds and hearts.

Now, in this new life, position defines us rather than sacrifice or performance. Isn't it interesting how, just like Adam and Eve in the garden, we keep trying to earn something we already have? We already have the position "child of God…beloved…complete in Him," but we keep performing or heaping guilt on because want to *feel* as if we deserve our position in Christ or because we don't even recognize our position at all! Instead of all this striving, we can enjoy the worth Jesus gives us instead of trying to create our own.

What About Condemnation?

> So now the case is closed. There remains no accusing voice of condemnation against those who are joined in life-union with Jesus, the Anointed One.
>
> Romans 8:1

There is no condemnation anymore. None! Not one bit (Romans 8:1). I think most of us think of condemnation externally, as in someone telling us that we don't measure up or aren't worthy. While that can happen, what is even worse is when we do this to ourselves.

We internalize all the messages we have received throughout our lives, messages of worthlessness, betrayal, abandonment, and failure. When we absorb these as part of our identity, we feel condemned constantly. Nothing we do or say can be right, and we obsess over every word or action by trying to fix them and get them right.

Even worse, religion tells us we *should* receive condemnation. Religion tells us we should beat ourselves up because it will help us do better. And we should believe that we are always one step away from abject failure and rejection by God. This just isn't true!

Religion, though, always results in our trying to use our resources (or lack thereof) to get it right before a displeased god. It is about what we can do to make God happy, and from the religious mindset, He is not an easy one to please. God's Word, however, says something completely different: there is no condemnation for us in Jesus.

Breaking Free

It is His job to keep us, to complete His work, and to provide the resources we need to live in relationship with Him (Philippians 1:6). Abiding in Him is not living under condemnation, but rather rejoicing in the freedom He brings from religion.

So, the only accusing voice of condemnation that remains is the one we allow. It is the voice of trying to achieve something we already have. It is the voice that drives us to an unattainable goal. Unattainable, because with Jesus's Life within, we already have everything we need. Jesus did not just die for us (an amazing gift of love and sacrifice), but He also lives with us continually (Matthew 28:20). He does not live with us as a constant condemning voice, but rather one that calls us to Himself to live out of the abundance He provides for each day.

He is not waiting for us to achieve a standard. He has already met the standard and will continue to do so through us. If you are receiving condemnation, it is NOT from Jesus. So, don't continue to condemn yourself when Jesus Himself does not.

How About Renewing Your Mind?

> Stop imitating the ideals and opinions of the culture around you, but be inwardly transformed by the Holy Spirit through a total reformation of how you think. This will empower you to discern God's will as you live a beautiful life, satisfying and perfect in his eyes.
> Romans 12:2

Finally, there is the renewing of our minds based on the new life we have. When Jesus gives us His life for ours, transferring us from death to life and making us new creations, He makes our spirits alive (Ephesians 2:1–5). Our spirits were dead and needed to be breathed back to life. I think I expected that to mean my mind would also be free of all the junk of the past. But, while the initial transfer of life is instantaneous, an opening of a door, the renewing of our minds takes a bit longer and is a process.

The difference is that we now have a choice. Before we receive new life from Jesus, we have only the usual system—we feel controlled by negative identity messages, trying to change and improve ourselves. We look for a way to somehow cope with life because the system is failing us, and then we feel all those negative identity messages twice as severely. It's not a great system, but it's the only one we have, so we keep trying to make it work.

In the religious paradigm, we are trying to keep ourselves from sinning, obsessively working to change our thought patterns and to keep ourselves on the straight-and-narrow. In living the abiding life, all of this is up to God's work in our lives. We are not responsible for renewing our minds but rather for looking to Him to do so for us. We recognize we cannot do this ourselves, and trying to just exasperates us and often leads us back into deeper brain spirals. Jesus is the Renewer of our minds, and only in relationship with Him will our minds change in this way.

When we receive new life, we reorient ourselves by stopping the cycle and recognizing the messages as untrue. The process of discerning truth from lies and allowing God to change our neuron pathways is how I would define renewing your mind. We will talk more about this throughout the coming chapters, but for now, know that a renewed mind results from this new life we have in Jesus, and it is not something we know how to do on our own. God oversees renewing our minds, and He will keep doing it. However, life becomes so much more fun when we participate in that change.

How do we participate? By saying "yes." Sounds simple, but God is a gentleman and does not force us to do anything. When we agree with the renewing of our mind, we allow a way to change that we could not even imagine. Perspectives can shift, depression can lift, and our view on life can move from death to life. Our spirits have already moved, but our minds can follow as well.

Some feel their love-receivers are broken and may wonder how they can receive love from God. So many have experienced significant pain in their lives that makes them feel as though they could never receive love from any being, least of all God. I do not believe we can fix this—but we can ask Him to do so.

When my kids have broken toys (which is almost daily), they have learned to gather up the pieces of the precious item and take it to my husband for mending. As a result, their father has become an expert in gluing together items that seem beyond repair. He does this using special glue and a system of various weights to keep the pieces stuck together. This is how I picture God dealing with our love-receivers. All that is required of us is to gather up the broken pieces of our hearts and lay them in the lap of Jesus, allowing Him to fix them as only He can.

Make yourself available for healing in this process. So many times, throughout the Gospels, Jesus asked if someone really wanted to get well. I think the underlying question was, what are you willing to give up in order to be healed? Is it self-protection, pride, control (or the illusion of it), or just not being willing to come to Jesus in the first place? If you don't trust Him, that's ok. But be honest and tell Him that. Bring the broken pieces of your heart to Him and leave them with the Master Mender. He is able to renew your mind, restore your soul, and bring joy to your life right now as you live the abiding life in relationship with Him.

Going Deeper

1. How have you made salvation about performance rather than receiving Love's pursuit of you?

2. Are there any ways you are still living as an orphan rather than receiving your adoption and God's love for you as a fact?

3. Spend some time soaking in the incredible love that God the Father, the Son, and the Holy Spirit have for you. Here are some verses to meditate on, keeping in mind that these refer to God's love for and in us, not about anything we should attempt to accomplish:

> *So now I live with the confidence that there is nothing in the universe with the power to separate us from God's love. I'm convinced that his love will triumph over death, life's troubles, fallen angels, or dark rulers in the heavens. There is nothing in our present or future circumstances*

that can weaken his love. There is no power above us or beneath us— no power that could ever be found in the universe that can distance us from God's passionate love, which is lavished upon us through our Lord Jesus, the Anointed One!

Romans 8:38–39

Love is large and incredibly patient. Love is gentle and consistently kind to all. It refuses to be jealous when blessing comes to someone else. Love does not brag about one's achievements nor inflate its own importance. Love does not traffic in shame and disrespect, nor selfishly seek its own honor. Love is not easily irritated or quick to take offense. Love joyfully celebrates honesty and finds no delight in what is wrong. Love is a safe place of shelter, for it never stops believing the best for others. Love never takes failure as defeat, for it never gives up.

1 Corinthians 13:4–6

Love never brings fear, for fear is always related to punishment. But love's perfection drives the fear of punishment far from our hearts. Whoever walks constantly afraid of punishment has not reached love's perfection.

1 John 4:18

Then, by constantly using your faith, the life of Christ will be released deep inside you, and the resting place of his love will become the very source and root of your life. Then you will be empowered to discover what every holy one experiences—the great magnitude of the astonishing love of Christ in all its dimensions. How deeply intimate and far-reaching is his love! How enduring and inclusive it is! Endless love beyond measurement that transcends our understanding—this extravagant love pours into you until you are filled to overflowing with the fullness of God!

Ephesians 3:17–19

But you, O Lord, your mercy-seat love is limitless, reaching higher than the highest heavens. Your great faithfulness is infinite, stretching over the whole earth. Your righteousness is unmovable, just like the mighty mountains. Your judgments are as full of wisdom as the oceans are full of water. Your tender care and kindness leave no one forgotten, not a man or even a mouse. O God, how extravagant is your cherishing love! All mankind can find a hiding place under the shadow of your wings.

Psalm 36:5–7

And this hope is not a disappointing fantasy, because we can now experience the endless love of God cascading into our hearts through the Holy Spirit who lives in us!

Romans 5:5

Hannah Morrell

Abiding

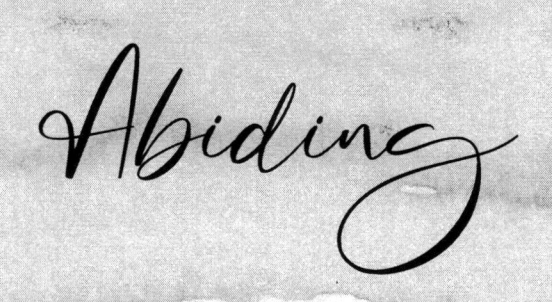

> "The Christian life is not difficult; it is impossible. Jesus is the only man who ever lived it, and the only way we will ever live it is if He lives it through us."
>
> —Mike Wells[4]

We have acknowledged that God's great love has pursued relationship with us by bringing salvation and restoration to us through Jesus. But then what? I think often Christians stop at this point and no longer receive Life as a grace but rather as a checklist they must perform for the remainder of their time on earth. That's why there are so many people in the camp of slogging it out until heaven—some have termed this being a "suicidal rapturist." Basically, you feel you must keep showing up for the drudgery of the day, but you can't kill yourself because that's not okay with God. Instead, you are continuously waiting until you can leave this earth through rapture or death (of natural causes rather than your own hand), and every day is just a consistent desire for the end.

I think we are missing the point of life on earth by existing in this way. I know the world can be a miserable place, but

---

[4] Wells, Mike. "Fundamentals of Abiding Life: Session #4." *Basic Seminar DVD Study Notes*. Abiding Life Ministries International. 16. https://abidinglife.com/pages/freeresources

sometimes the misery is of our own making. And regardless of the misery, we can choose to find joy when we see Jesus throughout our day. What I want is to know Jesus, the Way, the Truth, and the Life, by growing my relationship with Him while I'm experiencing this life. There is no separation. Life is already present, and I don't have to wait until heaven for it.

This is what we call abiding—living in moment-by-moment relationship with God rather than trying to follow the rules to hopefully make God happy.

What Is Abiding?

"I am the sprouting vine and you're my branches. As you live in union with me as your source, fruitfulness will stream from within you—but when you live separated from me you are powerless."
John 15:5

Abiding is one of those terms that can be confusing. Is it remaining? Is it passive? What do I actually do in order to abide? First, let's hear about abiding from a couple of other voices:

> To "abide" ...means to keep in fellowship with Christ so that His life can work in us and through us to produce fruit.
>
> —Warren Wiersbe[5]

> If, in our orthodox churches, the abiding in Christ, the living union with Him, the experience of His daily and hourly presence and keeping, were preached with the same distinctness and urgency as His atonement and pardon through His blood, I am confident that many would be found to accept with gladness the invitation to such a life, and that its influence would be manifest in their experience of the purity and the power, the love and the

---
5 Wiersbe, Warren W. *Be Transformed (John 13-21): Christ's Triumph Means Your Transformation*. Colorado Springs, CO: Cook, 2008, 41.

joy, the fruit-bearing, and all the blessedness which the Saviour connected with the abiding in Him.

—Andrew Murray[6]

❀ If Christians got as excited about staying connected to Christ as we did about coming to him in the first place, we'd experience more power. We'd feel more joy. We'd become people of impact. The deepest cry of our souls— for an encounter with Jesus that will sustain us even when our hearts fail and our prayers feel empty and flat—would be satisfied.

—Jodie Berndt[7]

I think in defining abiding, a metaphor helps, and it's actually a metaphor Jesus used in John 15:5 about the Vine and the branches. Imagine a branch which decides that it can produce grapes just fine on its own—it doesn't need the sustenance it receives by being attached to Vine. The pressure gets even worse as the branch believes the Vine has required it to produce fruit and feels condemnation as it isn't feeling up to the task. You can see the branch will get frustrated, blame the Vine for putting this standard on it, and finally grow completely discouraged, assuming it can never live fruitfully and content as it was created to live.

This picture describes so many Christians who have received Christ and His incredible love for them but then have decided it is up to them to live according to the standards He has set. The pressure mounts, the frustration grows, and no fruit develops. So, they find plastic fruit (or religious effort) and decorate their leaves with it, hoping that it will look like the real thing.

---

6 Murray, Andrew. "Preface," *Abide in Christ: Thoughts on the Blessed Life of Fellowship with the Son of God*. Philadelphia, PA: The Rodgers Company, 1888, 4.
7 Berndt, Jodie. "What Does It Mean to Abide?" *BibleGateway Blog*. June 1, 2021. https://www.biblegateway.com/blog/2021/06/what-does-it-means-to-abide/

We try to please God with all sorts of obedience and commitments, while He is offering to empower us to live with real fruitfulness. Instead, we decide it is up to us on our own and continue to put out the plastic fruit. Eventually, hopelessness and discouragement follow, but we must also hold others to the same standards we have set for ourselves in order to keep up the charade.

Believe me, I don't mean to criticize those who find themselves in this position, having been there myself. I played the performance-for-God game and lost. I became discouraged, bitter, and angry because I thought God required something of me but that He didn't provide what I needed to fulfill His requirement. It was all I could do to keep up with the plastic fruit.

But this isn't the abiding life. This isn't the life union with Jesus that is promised in Scripture.

Imagine again with me this same branch, who finally decides that it needs to recognize the union it has with the Vine. It sees that its attempts at fruitfulness have been disastrous, and it longs for something more. As it lives, acknowledging its union with the Vine as its source, it becomes fruitful. Suddenly, there are delicious grapes, sweet with the beautiful lifeblood of the Vine flowing into the branch. The branch is not trying harder to bear fruit or criticizing itself into fruit production. It is resting. It is allowing the

> HE BRINGS US TO HIMSELF, GIVES US A NEW LIFE, AND THEN GIVES US EVERYTHING WE NEED TO PLEASE HIM IN LIVING IT.

fruitfulness of the union with the Vine to stream from within to be enjoyed by all around it.

We are *not* called to a life of greater performance. We are *not* called to a life of comparison. We are *not* called to a life of discouragement and condemnation.

We *are* called to a union, something we crave so deeply. We get to live in union with Jesus through His Spirit within us, Who provides all we need for fruitfulness. He brings us to Himself, gives us a new Life, and then gives us everything we need to please Him in living it!

Abiding life is one of relationship and intimacy unlike anything we can have with humans because God also provides everything we require to live and be fruitful as He works through us. Our focus is no longer worshipping the rules and formulas in an attempt to create fruit but worshipping God Himself as He produces fruit through us.

I believe abiding is the place where we can move from being defeated, frustrated, religious Christians to a place of rest, peace, and trust. The Christian life is not meant to just be a free gift of salvation, followed by the presentation of an extensive list of things to do and not do.

I find it quite discouraging to go from this amazing new Life we've received and new creation we become, this new relationship where we can access God directly in a way we never thought possible, to the collision with religious rules that are supposed to teach us to live up to the gift we have received. Spoiler alert—we can't! And God knew we could not, which is why He has not only died to make us new and to adopt us as children but has also come to live with us. He empowers us to live the Christian Life. He gives it all!

When I was first working with my friend and mentor Mike Wells, he sent me to Honduras to do a conference all by myself through a translator. It was for a group of pastors from around the country, and I was a little 20-something kid who was supposed to teach them counseling and abiding. I did pretty well with most of the lectures, teaching them lots about counseling, flesh patterns, and personality. But I didn't recognize the importance of abiding, and so I covered it only briefly. My sweet friend Debbie (who is now in heaven rejoicing with Jesus face-to-face and cancer-free) was the missionary I was working with in Honduras, and she asked me to go over the abiding part again in my last session.

To this day, I know I didn't do it justice, but I also know that she was able to teach it to many in that room over the years because she knew abiding. She also knew that without moment-by-moment dependence on the Life of Christ within, we are just teaching information without power. It took years before I learned the importance of abiding as I wearied of trying to be my own source for life.

As a brief aside, did you know that you have a divine janitor? Mike Wells used to talk about how in Psalm 23, God's goodness and tender love follow you all the days of your life, so you don't have to worry about the messes you make as you go. The divine janitor is at work cleaning up all of those and bringing beauty and restoration. I find that incredibly helpful when I want to dwell in regret over choices or mistakes. Even my immaturity in being unable to share the importance of abiding was cleaned up behind me by the One who can bring good out of any situation.

Abiding changes the way we do life entirely, provides a chance for rest while moving, and releases us from the prison of religion.

A New Way of Life

> "My old identity has been co-crucified with Christ and no longer lives. And now the essence of this new life is no longer mine, for the Anointed One lives his life through me—we live in union as one! My new life is empowered by the faith of the Son of God who loves me so much that he gave himself for me, dispensing his life into mine!"
> Galatians 2:20

Abiding is a new pattern of living, a choosing of a different source. We have been made new creations (2 Corinthians 5:17), so we have access to a new Source. Before this resurrection Life, we had only our own flesh from which to pull resources. Our flesh is a pattern of living which includes attempting to change the messages we believe about ourselves and coping when life gets too much. This old pattern is comfortably uncomfortable. We know it doesn't work, but it's what we've always done, so we keep trying to make it work.

God does not force us to abide, or to choose to live out of His resources instead of our own. He is a gentleman and forces nothing on us. He waits until we are ready. When we choose—

there is really no strength in a choice—we consciously look to something else for help rather than remaining where we are.

Abiding requires humility and faith rather than pride and unbelief. Mike Wells often said that a lot of us live as "unbelieving believers." That means we have understood and accepted salvation through Christ, but that's where it stopped. I really like how Dan Stone describes this in his book *Rest of the Gospel*. He says once Christians experience salvation, if they do not go further with the Life of Christ, that's all they have to talk about. They just keep harping on sin and salvation rather than moving into the rest of the gospel, which is how to live the Christian life. God does not just give us a new life and leave us to figure it out on our own!

So, we get to look to Jesus as a Source, choosing to ask Him for enough to live life, as well as enough to save us from death. We are not just saved for the future, but Christ's Life is present and active today and right now. Abiding life allows us to live without the discouragement that religion brings as we try so hard to live a life that is only possible as we live in union with Christ.

Breaking Free
Completeness

> *"For he is the complete fullness of deity living in human form. And our own completeness is now found in him. We are completely filled with God as Christ's fullness overflows within us. He is the Head of every kingdom and authority in the universe!"*
>
> Colossians 2:9–10

In addition to having a new Source from which to draw strength and to meet all your needs, you have also been made complete in Him. Abiding is the state of being that recognizes the completeness, that there is nothing else we need to do or be in order to be in union with Christ because He has already done it all.

Complete does not mean we look perfect. I believe we are being perfected in Christ, but we still have some cracks. I love the concept of the Japanese art of kintsugi. It is an art form in which broken pottery is pieced together and sealed with molten gold, producing a beauty that was not previously apparent. The gold is not used to conceal cracks; rather, it makes them more pronounced as they shine forth from the pottery. The vessel is once again complete, but it is obvious the gold holds it together in a new way. With the gold of Jesus' love, the cracks of our own lives are obvious, but beautiful.

When we recognize the beauty of completeness in Him rather than fighting to achieve it on our own, we can relax. I once heard a story about two people who embarked on a cross-country flight. One was a businessman, a frequent flyer who was very comfortable with the situation. He found his seat, opened his newspaper (this old story pre-dates Kindles and laptops), and enjoyed his flight with a snack and drink. The other traveler was an elderly grandmother en route to visit her grandchildren. She had never been on a plane before and was terrified. She timidly found her seat, buckled her seatbelt tightly, and gripped the arms of the seat during the entire trip. The woman sat sweating and trembling, and being totally consumed by a fear of crashing, she could not bring herself to even accept a drink of water.

These two people disembarked at the same destination after riding in the same plane with the same pilot. They both arrived safely. Upon landing, however, their states of mind were incredibly different. The man, who trusted the pilot and was accustomed to the ride, was relaxed and ready for his meetings at the other end. The woman, who did not trust the pilot and feared every bump and sway of the plane, arrived barely able to walk because she was so stressed.

When we choose to see our completeness and trust the Pilot's leadership, we can move through life with much less stress. If we believe it is our job to worry enough to keep our plane in the air, we cannot function well, and we live in a constant state of anxiety. Abiding life is a much more restful place from which to operate, recognizing we are complete and have all we need to live life in relationship with God (2 Peter 1:3).

Breaking Free
Abiding and Weakness

> *"But he answered me, 'My grace is always more than enough for you, and my power finds its full expression through your weakness.' So I will celebrate my weaknesses, for when I'm weak I sense more deeply the mighty power of Christ living in me. So I'm not defeated by my weakness, but delighted! For when I feel my weakness and endure mistreatment—when I'm surrounded with troubles on every side and face persecution because of my love for Christ—I am made yet stronger. For my weakness becomes a portal to God's power."*
> 2 Corinthians 12:9–10

Although we are made complete and have all we need for life, abiding doesn't mean our human weakness goes away. In the verses above, Paul speaks of celebrating his weakness, not hiding or condemning it. I have witnessed Christians often try to show up to a social gathering with each person pretending they have no weakness, no burden, no problems. What a disservice this does to the body of Christ! We end up feeling as if we must be wrong somehow for having some areas in our lives that are so troubling that they make us feel as if we are living in a hell of our own making.

God doesn't just save us from future hell but from today's hell. That means abiding becomes the recognition of what He does in my present, everyday scenarios. He promises to not just give us new Life, but to give us the power to do today. He provides everything we need (Philippians 4:19).

He promises to fully satisfy every need we have. To accept His strength in our weakness, we must first acknowledge our weakness. He already knows we are failing, so coming to terms with our lack is really about our pride rather than His knowledge. Sometimes we don't want to admit to ourselves that we don't have enough for the situation. But when our tenacity wears thin and we come to a place where we can no longer function, we finally recognize we are too weak.

My friend, Mike Wells, used to wake up and tell God that today was already too big for him before he had even gotten out of bed. He asked Jesus to come and be all that he needed. That meant his everything. What a sweetness and relief there is in ceasing to try harder to meet a standard that is really impossible in our own strength and come to accept all the provision God brings for our every moment of every day. We can admit our weakness anytime throughout the day, accepting that He is enough for everything that is coming.

We may not like how He provides, by the way. I do believe He will provide, but it may not be in the way we expect or desire. Last year, my word for the year was "receive." I wanted to focus on learning to receive God's gifts, even when they weren't what I expected. I had planned a women's retreat and had prayed for more women to sign up to make it financially viable. I kept praying for more women, but more did not come. I feared maybe I had finally hit a point where God had ceased to provide. I had to call the hotel to find out if I could give back some of the reserved rooms, as we weren't going to fill them. Wouldn't you know it? The hotel was completely booked for that weekend and was more than happy to take back some rooms from my reserved block without leaving me financially responsible for them! We could still have a smaller retreat with the women God brought for the time. I had been praying for Him to make a way, but I had an expectation of how He would do that. Instead, He provided exactly as He knew best. I needed to learn to receive the gift as provided by His best plan, rather than push away God's provision because it didn't happen as I thought it should.

I had also prayed for family time and rest in early 2022 after a very busy holiday season with lots going on. My family all ended up with COVID in January, which gave us some very concentrated family time and a week of rest. Again, not how I would have expected or requested it, but He brought what we needed. I want to, more and more, learn to receive the gifts as He brings them and not turn my nose up at them because they are not in the packaging I expected.

God has promised to provide for your needs and be enough through you for every situation. This doesn't mean you will live in comfort or that you will agree with the way God accomplishes this. Abiding means that you do not have to fear or hide weakness; instead, you can celebrate it as a portal to God's power through you.

The Result of Abiding

"But the fruit produced by the Holy Spirit within you is divine love in all its varied expressions: joy that overflows, peace that subdues, patience that endures, kindness in action, a life full of virtue, faith that prevails, gentleness of heart, and strength of spirit. Never set the law above these qualities, for they are meant to be limitless."
Galatians 5:22-23

The result of abiding is fruit of the Spirit that pours out of your life naturally because it moves through you as a branch on the Vine. I think the prevailing implication that we are doing something wrong is if we are drumming up our own joy in a rough situation, our own faith for believing something that seems impossible, or our own kindness for the jerks of the world. These are things we cannot accomplish on our own; this is the fruit of the SPIRIT. That means it is a natural outflow of the Holy Spirit within us, not something we need to work hard to generate. It is all a result of the Spirit working within us.

I love gardening—well, I sometimes love gardening. Spring is the best time for a gardener, as there is an anticipation of harvest no matter how the year before went. The harvest is great fun and delicious as well. But, as I walk through my little garden, I never hear the plants grunting and groaning in an effort to produce fruit. The fruits and vegetables are a natural outflow of the plants as they stay rooted in the soil receiving sun and water. This is our Life. God is not a tough taskmaster whom we disappoint as we strain and strive to please Him. Instead, He holds our hand and guides us, leading us in Life and bringing sweet relief and strength in our weakness, celebrating the fruit that He Himself brings forth through us. What a deal!

Going Deeper:

1. Are there areas of your life for which you believe you must generate your own strength, that everything is up to you?

2. Ask the Father to reveal the transformation in you that happens when you see Him as the source of your strength

instead of your own resourcefulness, intelligence, education, etc.

3. What are the areas of your life in which you need to release control and admit weakness so that you can see God meet your needs in them?

4. Think about times in your life when you have tried to generate your own fruit and ask the Holy Spirit to be your source of fruit for today.

Hannah Morrell

Your Past & Flesh Pattern

"So many of our deepest longings to succeed are really just ways to be for ourselves what Christ should be for us. Really we are saying, 'If I achieve this, then I am acceptable!' But when we stop trying to steal self-acceptance from other sources, we lose our fear. We become fearless without becoming defiant."

—Tim Keller[8]

At this point, you may have a question or two. For instance, if you are indeed a new creation and have the Life of Christ constantly available to empower and guide you, why do you keep sinning? And why do you not feel free from your past or the incessant voice in your head telling you how much of a loser you are? Why can't you live the abiding life constantly?

Although you are a new creation with a spirit alive to the Life of Christ, you still have a suitcase in your head carrying the pain of the past, the methods of coping in the past, and the voice of judgement recorded in your head over many years. I call this the flesh. The flesh is really a dead person we carry around with us, thinking we can make it alive again. Galatians 2:20 is fairly clear that our old nature and the ways we have

---

[8] Keller, Timothy. *The Prodigal Prophet: Jonah and the Mystery of God's Mercy.* United States, Penguin Publishing Group, 2018.

tried to live life are crucified with Christ, and now we live a new life in Him. The remnants of this old life tend to stick around, though, and it can be difficult to recognize they don't work.

When my friend Mike died, his body was prepared in Costa Rica because that's where he took his final earthly breaths. We went to the viewing after his body had been flown back from Costa Rica, and I was horrified to see they had put so much makeup on his face that he was nearly unrecognizable. I knew I was supposed to be somber, but I couldn't help but giggle thinking of his comments if he had seen his body lying there. Now, if I propped his body up and acted as though he had never died, this would be equivalent to what we do with our flesh. The person is dead, but the baggage is still lying around, and we try to make it work for daily life.

A flesh pattern is the method you use to make life work without Christ. This starts with the negative identity messages ingrained from the time of your childhood through present day, which tell you that you are inadequate, unloved, dirty, used, guilty, a failure, etc. Nobody wants to feel as if these are true about themselves, so we must come up with ways to deal with these.

Attempts at Self-Improvement

"Great sorrow awaits you religious scholars and Pharisees—frauds and imposters! You are nothing more than tombs painted over with white paint—tombs that look shining and beautiful on the outside but filled with rotting corpses on the inside."
Matthew 23:27

Breaking Free

In dealing with flesh pattern baggage and negative identity messages it contains, we first try to change the messages by improving ourselves. These are not bad or evil attempts, but they are ineffective. We might try working harder, receiving more education, getting married (sometimes more than once), moving, attending church, getting involved in a ministry, or loving harder. Often this becomes a religious focus, worshipping the rules the religious leaders have set for you in order to improve yourself and not feel bad anymore. It doesn't matter what kind of makeup you add to the outside of a dead body; you are not making it more alive. You are not changing anything really—you are just covering up what is there. So, our attempts to change ourselves do not work the way we wish they would.

In the verse above, Jesus calls out the religious leaders of His day who created a façade behind which they hid the death and evil inside themselves. Polishing up the outside and condemning everyone who didn't seem to meet their standard was their self-improvement technique, and modern religious circles often use the same methods. Jesus is quick to call them out with extreme words, comparing their insides with rotting corpses! He is telling them that no matter how polished the outside looks, God looks at the heart (1 Samuel 16:7), and their self-improvement didn't change them in the way they thought it did.

When I was in high school, I remember being approached by a woman in a church one day. She told me she wanted her daughter to grow up to be just like me, and I smiled and thanked her. Inside my head, though, there was a raging scream. "Please don't do that!" I thought. Outside, I had dressed up my image with all the trappings—I performed well. I did ministry, and I worked really hard. Inside, though, I still felt completely worthless and was struggling with suicidal thoughts. No matter how much I added to the outside, I could not get the inside of me to reflect anything good. I didn't know peace until I quit trying to make my life work my way.

> SELF-IMPROVEMENT IS A FLESH PATTERN WE USE TO NAVIGATE LIFE WITHOUT ABIDING IN CHRIST BUT IT DOESN'T GIVE US THE DESIRED RESULT.

Self-improvement is not abiding life. In it, we try to fuel our own fire, so to speak. We clean up our own externals to look like we think will be acceptable, while inside, we feel rotten and continue to struggle with negative identity messages. These attempts to change don't get rid of the yucky voice that speaks so horribly to us inside our brains. Self-improvement is a flesh pattern we use to navigate life without abiding in Christ, but it doesn't give us the desired result.

Coping

"My people are guilty of a double sin: they have abandoned me, the Spring of Living Water, and they have dug for themselves cisterns—cracked cisterns that hold no water."
Jeremiah 2:13

After the attempts to change don't do what we want them to do, we must cope to survive. Coping is an attempt to remove pain in pursuit of a little pleasure. Coping can be pretty or ugly, but it's still trying to deal with life on our own. It could include anything from withdrawing and shutting down, to lashing out and manipulating, to substance abuse or sex. The reduction of pain and receipt of pleasure only lasts for a second, though, and ends up pushing us further into trying to "prove" our identity messages. Things like:

- When we withdraw, and no one follows, we really must be alone and abandoned by everyone.
- When we lash out, we must be jerks, and something must really be wrong with us.
- When we abuse substances and sex, we must be dirty and rejected and ashamed.

Each method of coping just leads us further into the mess of feeling miserable and awful, compounding all the messages we have heard from the past.

Coping is really another word for an idol. Idols are things we worship to try to make life work.

I used to think the Israelites were so silly in the Old Testament. They got to see amazing miracles like the Red Sea parting and water coming out of rocks, but then when they ran into a problem, they cut down a tree and made an idol out of the wood, or they melted down their earrings to make an idol out of the gold. They created an object, and then they bowed down and worshipped it as if it were something other than a block of wood or a blob of melted gold.

But don't I do the same thing? I have tried the idol of performance so many times I've lost count, and I know it's hollow, dead, and unable to help me. But I still go back to it, hoping this time maybe it will save me and make me feel better. I am exactly like the Israelites. I want to control what saves me, so I go to something I know and feel I can control.

This flesh pattern of feeling the identity messages, attempting to improve myself, and then coping (which leads us back to feeling the messages on an even deeper level) seems normal, and we are accustomed to doing life this way. But it doesn't work. Without having Christ and His Life within us, this is the only option. It's the only way to try to muddle through life on our own. It is damaging, though, and further compounds this awful feeling that we are hopeless and stuck.

Identity Messages

> "But Christ proved God's passionate love for us by dying in our place while we were still lost and ungodly! And there is still so much more to say of his unfailing love for us! For through the blood of Jesus we have heard the powerful declaration, 'You are now righteous in my sight.' And because of the sacrifice of Jesus, you will never experience the wrath of God."
>
> Romans 5:8–9

We also keep going back to this pattern because we think we have proven the identity messages to be true in our heads. So now, we think we must prove them wrong before we can get out of them. If I believe I am a worthless failure, I have to "make something of myself" through career, money, power, or marriage in order to prove somehow that I am not a worthless failure. The problem is that this "proof" doesn't work and doesn't change the way I feel inside. No matter what I add to the outside, it doesn't fix or dismiss the negative identity messages that rule and control me.

Also, Jesus has already shown that this proving does not work. He has placed worth on our lives, whether we acknowledge it or not. But this was not because of something we did right. God has called us to Himself, while we were lost and ungodly. He has declared us righteous, free, and worthy. We keep trying to make our own way when He *is* the Way and is waiting for us to walk in Him.

I have talked to people from many walks of life with various past events that have shaped their identity messages. I think what we miss sometimes is that our current mess has a lot more to do with the messages we received than the actual events themselves. I am not negating the events or the pain we experienced because of the old messages, but we tend to react to current events that bring similar messages, rather than because we are experiencing the exact event again. This is why we may end up confused about something that sets off an alarm in our head when it doesn't seem remotely similar to an actual experience in our lives. It does, however, trigger a warning because the messages being communicated are similar.

I moved to Mexico for a few months after I completed my undergraduate degree. Really, I had no clue what to do with a humanities degree and thought maybe I would be a missionary in Mexico. I lived with a very sweet family and worked with a man who ran clubs for kids down in a dangerous part of Monterrey.

We would take the train down in the morning before the gang members woke up and make sure we left before noon to avoid those same individuals. The kids loved the attention and time we spent with them, and I enjoyed that part of the work.

While in Mexico, my wallet was stolen in a Walmart one day, right after I had withdrawn money from an ATM to cover my rent. I remember feeling as if my whole world was crashing down. I knew that calling the police was pointless, and my credit cards and cash were irretrievable. What was most interesting to me later, as I thought about this event, was that it wasn't that I felt unsafe, but I felt like a failure. I couldn't get it right, no matter how hard I tried. I had walked through incredibly dangerous parts of Monterrey, had learned to function in a new country, and wasn't really afraid ever—but this sense of failure reverberated deeply this experience of losing my wallet and security to a thief.

My identity messages were that I could never get it right, and I was failing. Because I measured my ability to be loved by my performance. As I sat outside the Walmart on the sidewalk, head in hands and tears streaming down my face, I felt as though a giant neon sign flashed above me: **Failure!!** When there is an event in my life, this is the message that most often still comes through.

Hurts of the past also affect different people according to their personalities. (The personality types I reference are from Mike Wells's Unique Self Test and include doer, thinker and feeler.)[9] The lens of personality affects every part of life. I

---
[9] Wells, Michael. *Unique Self Test*. Abiding Life Ministries International.

have seen a person who is a thinker (highly detailed, analytical, always thinking about something) react very differently to an abusive parent than a doer (driver, leader, bull-in-a-China-shop). The thinker will store up all the abuse, mentally obsessing over revenge, but never actually doing anything about it. They become more and more withdrawn, controlling everything in their environment they can and never being vulnerable to anyone for fear of being hurt again. Often, once they are out of the house, they have little or no contact with the abusive parent because their trust has been betrayed, and they do not feel safe. The identity messages they receive are that they are worthless, not good enough, and unimportant.

The doer, on the other hand, will wait until they are old enough or big enough to really let the abusive parent have it. They will physically or verbally fight back, putting the parent in their place and telling them never to mess with them again. They might also leave the house at a young age, determined to make their own way with no help from anyone. They might never give another thought to the parent, moving on and leaving problems behind. The identity messages the doer receives are that they were weak, stuck, and powerless—something they are determined never to be again.

Events don't really make us spin into a flesh pattern cycle. The messages behind the events are the real problem, but we often get distracted with coping or attempts to change that are more obvious to us. We must get behind the presenting problem to find the real problem.

What Do We Do with the Past?

> *"I don't depend on my own strength to accomplish this; however I do have one compelling focus: I forget all of the past as I fasten my heart to the future instead. I run straight for the divine invitation of reaching the heavenly goal and gaining the victory-prize through the anointing of Jesus."*
>
> Philippians 3:13–14

As we continue to identify the messages from the past, sometimes we obsess over events of the past that triggered identity messages. We can't get in a time machine and change the past, but focusing on the past like that does not fix it. In my role as a pastoral counselor, I find many people want to spend a lot of time on the past, hoping that talking about it will make it feel less painful. There is an obsession with "figuring it out" to bring relief. But focusing on the past does not make it okay or make sense.

> BUT FOCUSING ON THE PAST DOES NOT MAKE IT OKAY OR MAKE SENSE.

Even if we realize that someone hurt us because of their own painful past, it doesn't make the pain we experienced better or less painful. This is what I mean by figuring it out. We can understand that a parent was abused as a child, and that's why they abuse their own children. But that does not relieve the children, and it does not excuse the abuse.

I grew up in a farming community, and let me tell you, there is a lot of poop around. No farmer goes out and sits in a pile of poop to make sense of their livestock. They'd only get smelly and dirty but learn nothing. I realize it's a simplification, but that's essentially what we do when we obsess over the past and hope it's going to make a difference in our present and future. I do look at the past and its pain to find a way forward for now, but we must be careful not to get too fixated on it. I believe work on the past events of your life can allow you to turn pain into a steppingstone to help you move forward. That is always the focus, rather than trying to make sense out of something that doesn't make sense.

What Do We Do With the Flesh?

> "Jesus said to all of his followers, 'If you truly desire to be my disciple, you must disown your life completely, embrace my "cross" as your own, and surrender to my ways.'"
>
> Luke 9:23

Just as focusing on the past doesn't change it, focusing on the flesh pattern doesn't fix it. In fact, we are not trying to make the flesh stronger. It's a dead person, remember? So, when we get hung up on trying to make our flesh pattern work, we just get more and more stuck. The more we try to strengthen our willpower or generate our own self-control, the more we end up with even bigger problems because we cannot fix this flesh by ourselves.

Sometimes the terminology gets a little confusing in Scripture. I like the way Mike Wells's explanation of the three selves clarifies them for me.[10] There is the self you love (Mark 12:31) and were created to be, there is the self that died

---

10 Wells, Michael. "Feeler, Thinker, and Doer: Session #20." *Basic Seminar DVD Study Notes.* Abiding Life Ministries International. 91. https://abidinglife.com/pages/freeresources

(Gal 2:20) when it was crucified with Christ, and there's the self you deny (Luke 9:23), which is this flesh pattern we are addressing.

So, how do you deny or disown this self/flesh? First, recognize it is not true! These negative identity messages feel true but are not the Truth from God. When we accept the new Life that God has provided in Jesus, He takes our old crap (yes, that's what it is) and all our old messages and gives us new Life and new messages that are the Truth. We have been so used to living the old way that the new way feels weird and uncomfortable for a while. But you are not the messages of the past! God has freed you from those and given you a new identity as a new creation.

Next, get obsessive about the Truth! Look at what God says about you and speak that Truth when the little voice inside your head tries to go into the repeat cycle again. Tell that little voice to shut up. You have listened to it for too long, and it hasn't helped you. Here are a few Truths to get you started:

- You are a conqueror!

"Yet even in the midst of all these things, we triumph over them all, for God has made us to be more than conquerors, and his demonstrated love is our glorious victory over everything!"
Romans 8:37

- You are loved!

"So now I live with the confidence that there is nothing in the universe with the power to separate us from God's love. I'm convinced that his love will triumph over death, life's troubles, fallen angels, or dark rulers in the heavens. There is nothing in our present or future circumstances that can weaken his love."
Romans 8:38

Breaking Free

❃ You are accepted!

"Our faith in Jesus transfers God's righteousness to us and he now declares us flawless in his eyes. This means we can now enjoy true and lasting peace with God, all because of what our Lord Jesus, the Anointed One, has done for us. Our faith guarantees us permanent access into this marvelous kindness that has given us a perfect relationship with God. What incredible joy bursts forth within us as we keep on celebrating our hope of experiencing God's glory!"

Romans 5:1–2

❃ You are free!

"At last we have freedom, for Christ has set us free! We must always cherish this truth and firmly refuse to go back into the bondage of our past."

Galatians 5:1

❃ You are courageous!

"Do not yield to fear, for I am always near. Never turn your gaze from me, for I am your faithful God. I will infuse you with my strength and help you in every situation. I will hold you firmly with my victorious right hand."

Isaiah 41:10

What About Emotions?

"Stop imitating the ideals and opinions of the culture around you, but be inwardly transformed by the Holy Spirit through a total reformation of how you think. This will empower you to discern God's will as you live a beautiful life, satisfying and perfect in his eyes."

Romans 12:2

There will still be emotions tied to these negative identity messages you have been soaking in for so long. Feelings are not bad, but they need to be guided by Truth. Instead of being controlled by your emotions, you can use them as warning lights. Whenever you are listening to that little awful voice, you will experience certain emotions, and when you realize why you feel this way, you can stop yourself before you spiral too far. Every person has individual feelings when listening to their negative identity messages, but some of them are things like anger (feeling out of control with rage—some people actually see red), anxiety (shoulders tense, breathing shallow and fast, heart rate going up), or depression (as if a cold, wet blanket is dropped on your shoulders, and you ooze into the floor).

When you identify your feeling, you can check what you are believing and what started the feeling. I like to call it a rewind. Once you recognize the feeling, you can rewind your day (or days depending on how long you've been in the grip of the feeling) and realize what started this reaction. Then, speak Truth into that situation rather than just allowing the identity messages you've received there to take deeper root. These messages are not always vocally communicated, but you can receive them out of so many situations because they are already ingrained in you.

This re-recording of the voice in your head is what I would call renewing of your mind, and it is a slow and difficult process. But the good news is that this is God's job, and your job is just to be open to it. The freedom that results from this new focus on Truth, though, is addictive and so much better than trying to make the flesh pattern spin fast enough to work. Once you believe even a little of what God says about you,

> ONCE YOU BELIEVE EVEN A LITTLE OF WHAT GOD SAYS ABOUT YOU, THE INCREDIBLE LOVE GOD HAS FOR YOU WILL ENCOURAGE YOU DEEPLY AND BLOW YOU AWAY.

the incredible love God has for you will encourage you deeply and blow you away.

Why is the Flesh Still Around?

> "Are you weary, carrying a heavy burden? Come to me. I will refresh your life, for I am your oasis. Simply join your life with mine. *Learn my ways and you'll discover that I'm gentle, humble, easy to please.* You will find refreshment and rest in me."
> Matthew 11:28–29

So, why is the flesh left? Why not erase it all when Jesus defeated sin and death on the cross? I think sometimes we confuse eradication and defeat. Jesus took away the power sin and the flesh had over us, as well as the downfall that death dealt us. But sin, the flesh, and death are all still around and will be until the point at which God's Kingdom is fully revealed and we get to live in a new way entirely without the trappings of the old world.

I believe the purpose of the flesh is to drive us to Jesus. When we realize coping doesn't work, we must have some other direction to move in, rather than just coming up with a new coping mechanism. Remember, idols are just dead wood or metal, but people worship them everywhere still, just as they did in the Bible. It seems silly to think of someone making an idol and then turning to bow down to it. But we do the same thing every time we think our own idols are going to save us. We have manufactured them, and they are as useless as a block of wood.

Life actually gets very simple when you have this mindset. When you realize you are believing lies, come to Jesus. When you realize you are trying to make idols work, come to Jesus. When you feel discouraged because you went there again, come to Jesus. He will NEVER tire of your coming to Him. It's not about making our past or flesh pattern better, but more about turning from it and seeing we have a Way (John 14:6), we have Strength (Philippians 4:13), and we have a new Life in Christ (2 Corinthians 5:17).

Going Deeper:

1. What lies do the negative identity messages ingrained in your head tell you?

2. How do you attempt to change those messages, and how do you cope when it doesn't work?

3. As you examine your idols and the lies you believe, bring them to Jesus and offer them to Him in exchange for Truth and real power through His life.

4. Allow God to renew your mind as you soak in the Truth using some of the Scriptures given and others that God brings to you as necessary.

5. When you find yourself following your default flesh pattern, don't beat yourself up, but see it for what it is and move into the Spirit who empowers you to live differently.

Breaking Free

Hannah Morrell

How Do We Abide?

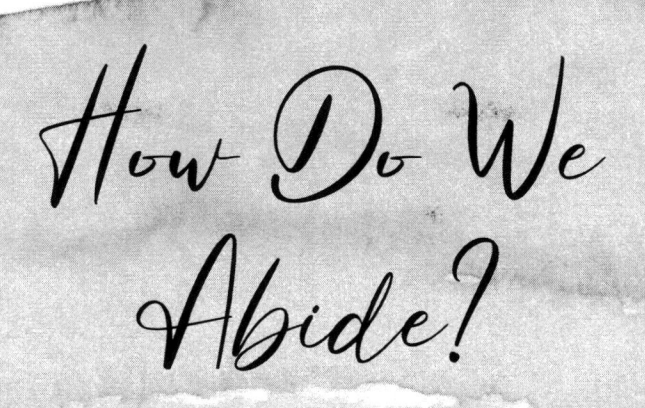

"While optimism makes us live as if someday soon things will go better for us, hope frees us from the need to predict the future and allows us to live in the present, with the deep trust that God will never leave us alone."

—Henri Nouwen[11]

Upon realizing the flesh pattern is not helping us and we need to turn from it and come to Jesus, how do we then live? John 15 talks about abiding, and the most often-asked question I hear is, "How do I abide?"

For many years, I convinced myself I could figure out the Christian life if I just tried harder. I really wanted love, but I used performance and productivity to get that love. I believed I was strong, and if I just kept working at it, I could live life in a way that made God proud of me. This led to a series of failures, which I believe God allowed to help me understand I could not do this myself. I got one degree and then another, but education didn't bring the life that I thought it would. I tried to be a missionary in Mexico and failed at that. I tried to be healthy and strong and wound up with an unexplained illness that left me unable to function for months.

---

11 Nouwen, Henri J. M. *The Dance of Life: Weaving Sorrows and Blessings Into One Joyful Step.* United Kingdom, Ave Maria Press, 2005.210.

I have come a long way in recognizing how weak I am since those years. And in that humility, I have realized how much I don't know! I am convinced now that the Christian life is only possible with the empowerment of God Himself, and that is what He offers as we exist as branches on the living Vine.

Admitting Where You Are...Honestly

"If you bow low in God's awesome presence, he will eventually exalt you as you leave the timing in his hands. Pour out all your worries and stress upon him and leave them there, for he always tenderly cares for you."

1 Peter 5:6–7

To abide, we start by admitting where we are. Are you weak, anxious, depressed, angry? You can stand in front of the little map in the mall all day long to find the store you want to go to, but if you don't know where you are, it's kind of pointless. You must know where you are before you know where you are going. I also think being honest with yourself and your God is so cathartic and healing. He can take it, so you might as well not pretend.

There are a few tools I like to use in this process. Sometimes when I am incredibly anxious or worried about juggling all the pieces of my life, I like to do a brain dump by writing everything I am thinking about to get it out of my head and onto paper (or an electronic format if you prefer). I read back through what I've written, and then I make a list of items I can actually do something about.

Breaking Free

With the rest, I think of Hezekiah in Isaiah 37:14, when he takes the threatening letter sent to him by an enemy army leader and spreads it out in front of the Lord with no idea of what to do. This is how I see my worries as I lay them out and entrust them to the God who holds me and the future. I don't know how to deal with them, but I am being honest about my worries, my fears, and my lack of trust.

Another tool I use is to look for what is and what is not in my control—and be honest here! I begin by confessing that I have a God, and I am not Him. I remember that no matter how much we worry about the future, we still have only an illusion of control, and we cannot prepare ourselves emotionally for what may come. We do not make a very good god, so we need to quit taking on His responsibility and thinking we will not suffer in doing so. Our shoulders are not big enough to take that on. There is very little we can dictate in our lives, and it definitely works much better to honor God and His power, as He is more than able to deal with it all.

> IN THE PAST—WE HAVE REGRET.
> IN THE FUTURE—WE HAVE WORRY.
> IN THE PRESENT—WE HAVE HOPE.

Sometimes we get to a point of admitting we can't do this life, and that's a point when things often can get very dark and even suicidal. We think the way out is to take away life, rather than recognizing our new one. To get past this place, we have to move one step further past our lack and see God's ability. He WILL do something. It may not be the something we wanted or thought He should do, but He will act. His action may be to continue to hold our heads above water rather than pulling us out of the ocean. But He will carry us. He says He will be all that we need (Philippians 4:19)—have you ever asked Him to prove it?

Returning to the Present

"Refuse to worry about tomorrow, but deal with each challenge that comes your way, one day at a time. Tomorrow will take care of itself."
Matthew 6:34

How else can you come to abiding? Return to the present. In the past—we have regret. In the future—we have worry. In the present—we have hope. Choose hope.

Mike Wells said that if we go into the past or future, we go without God, and it's incredibly overwhelming.[12] God is in the present, right now, and that's where abiding happens as we remain with Him.

I used to read Oswald Chambers' book *My Utmost for His Highest* and get quite frustrated with him, because I felt that the life he was encouraging was impossible. I think it took reading his biography to finally realize that Oswald struggled with depression and many other issues as he worked in ministry. He was not a perfect person but had a deep relationship with God, a practice of abiding, that allowed him to function during daily life. Here's what he had to say about it:

---

12 Wells, Michael. "Understanding Our Relationship to Christ: Session #24." *Basic Seminar DVD Study Notes.* Abiding Life Ministries International. 110. https://abidinglife.com/pages/freeresources

Breaking Free

> *"I have to get to the point of the absolute and unquestionable relationship that takes everything exactly as it comes from Him. God never guides us at some time in the future, but always here and now. Realize that the Lord is here now, and the freedom you receive is immediate."*
>
> —*Oswald Chambers*[13]

One reason we move into regret is we think we can make the flesh better by beating ourselves into not doing something stupid again. We act like the old monks who beat their backs with reeds until bloody, aiming to keep their minds from thoughts or actions they considered wrong. We try to do the same thing, only within our minds, and it does not improve the flesh. We must deny the flesh and recognize it for what it is—unhelpful! I like to imagine setting up a roadblock on those neuron pathways that lead to the place of regret. When I think… *if I had only made a different decision, moved to a different place, married a different person…* this is when I must reinforce my roadblock and remind myself that nothing good lies down that road. I am not fixing anything, and I'm just stealing any joy I could have in the present right now.

What's The Formula?

> *"Yahweh is my best friend and my shepherd. I always have more than enough. He offers a resting place for me in his luxurious love. His tracks take me to an oasis of peace near the quiet brook of bliss. That's where he restores and revives my life. He opens before me the right path and leads me along in his footsteps of righteousness so that I can bring honor to his name. Even when your path takes me through the valley of deepest darkness, fear will never conquer me, for you already have! Your authority is my strength and my peace. The comfort of your love takes away my fear. I'll never be lonely, for you are near. You become my delicious feast even when my enemies dare to fight.*

---

[13] Chambers, Oswald. *My Utmost for His Highest: Updated Language Paperback (A Daily Devotional with 366 Bible-Based Readings)*. Our Daily Bread Publishing, 2010. 55.

You anoint me with the fragrance of your Holy Spirit; you give me all I can drink of you until my cup overflows. So why would I fear the future? Only goodness and tender love pursue me all the days of my life. Then afterward, when my life is through, I'll return to your glorious presence to be forever with you!"

Psalm 23

I cannot tell you how many people have spent time in search of a formula for abiding. As if they were to say the right words or do the right dance, then they will be abiding. We cannot put a formula on something that is relational.

Often the formula we attempt is that of "doing the right thing" so that we get blessing. But we forget God has promised suffering, tribulation, and persecution in this world (John 16:33). Paul, the guy who was really doing exactly what God had called him to do, had a laundry list of ways he had suffered, and would continue to suffer during his imprisonment, and would later suffer execution because of his preaching. Perhaps we think we could try to control the future by our behavior today. But that is not the way God works it out. God did not base salvation on behavior—but we try to make it transactional! We think we can obey God into loving us, rather than understanding that obedience comes from being loved and desiring relationship with God. I think instead of a formula, abiding is about living dependent on the Life of Christ within us and acknowledging our lack of control and ability.

We are Christ's sheep, and He is our Shepherd (John 10:10). Being called a sheep is not a compliment, by the way. Sheep are definitely not smart. But they are great followers. Sometimes that gets them into trouble if they are following the wrong thing. Abiding is simply following the Shepherd. We

Breaking Free

get distracted and confused, but this is not news to God. He did not compare us to smart, independent animals like lions or dolphins. We are dependent, easily distracted, and needy. But He is happy to be our Shepherd and really enjoys us.

I heard of a man who was struggling with a lot of things in his life, and he decided to simply recite Psalm 23 all day long. There is so much power in this psalm, as we realize our roles as sheep and God's role as the Shepherd. I am including it above from the Passion Translation, one of my favorites.

One of the most impacting songs I have ever heard about blessing is that of Laura Story. I read her book *When God Doesn't Fix It* about her husband's brain tumor and the way her life has not turned out like she expected. Her song says:

> *We pray for blessings. We pray for peace. Comfort for family, protection while we sleep. We pray for healing, for prosperity. We pray for Your mighty hand to ease our suffering. All the while, You hear each spoken need, Yet love us way too much to give us lesser things.*
>
> *'Cause what if your blessings come through raindrops? What if Your healing comes through tears? What if a thousand sleepless nights are what it takes to know You're near? What if trials of this life are Your mercies in disguise?*
>
> *We pray for wisdom, Your voice to hear. We cry in anger when we cannot feel You near. We doubt your goodness; we doubt your love, as if every promise from Your Word is not enough. All the while, You hear each desperate plea and long that we'd have faith to believe.*
>
> *When friends betray us, when darkness seems to win, we know that pain reminds this heart that this is not our home.*
>
> *What if my greatest disappointments or the aching of this life is the revealing of a greater thirst this world can't satisfy? What if trials of this life, the rain, the storms, the hardest nights, are your mercies in disguise?*[14]

---

14 Story, Laura. "Blessings," *Blessings*. Track 5. Brentwood, TN: INO Records, 2011.

When we try to decide what we need or control God through our good behavior, we are in the wrong place with the wrong focus. Instead, we trade the formula for relationship. We can testify to blessing coming in all sorts of situations as our faithful Shepherd guides us through them faithfully.

Distractions and Anchors

> "Perfect, absolute peace surrounds those whose imaginations are consumed with you; they confidently trust in you. Yes, trust in the Lord Yahweh forever and ever! For Yahweh, the Lord God, is your Rock of Ages!"
>
> Isaiah 26:3–4

In abiding, we get to catch the distractions that are like flies buzzing around in our heads. The lies of who we are or who God is are those distractions—lies that feel true because they have been around for so long in our lives. Let the lies push you back to Jesus, asking Him for Truth. Anything that distracts us and steals our focus from Jesus is unhelpful. Even seemingly good things can be distractions that take us away from the place of abiding and accessing all that He has for us.

Sometimes, anchors are helpful as we seek to abide. Anchors are physical representations of intangible things. We are very forgetful and easily distracted, so God is faithful to provide areas that call us back to remembrance (Exodus 13:3–6; 24:4; Deuteronomy 27:1–8; Joshua 22:9–12; 24:24–28; 1 Samuel 7:12).

I have been rather clumsy my whole life, running into things, falling over things, and generally just bruising myself up everywhere I go. My husband baby-proofed the house for me, not the children. One day, when I was frustrated about getting hung up on a door handle while I went buzzing through the house to leave, God spoke and told me that this was one anchor He had provided to remind me. If, every time I get stuck, hurt, or tangled in something, I turn and thank Him for getting my attention and helping me come back, I gain a totally different perspective! He has provided many other anchors as well, because He knows I need lots of reminders. What are the anchors that help you remember God's presence in your daily life?

Moment by Moment

"For sin's meager wages is death, but God's lavish gift is life eternal, found in your union with our Lord Jesus, the Anointed One."
Romans 6:23

Abiding is a moment-by-moment walk, not a onetime fix. God has always wanted relationship, and this is part of His desire. We already have all we need, but we don't access it because we won't look to Him.

I once watched a K-9 dog perform with his handler at a festival. This dog was glued to the leg of his trainer, walking exactly in step with him as he went. The dog's head, however, was not looking forward, but craned back to look up at the face of his human, waiting for the signal to go. When his handler finally

> ABIDING IS A MOMENT-BY-MOMENT WALK, NOT A ONE-TIME FIX.

commanded him to go get the bad guy, he leaped into action, after which he returned to his position with the trainer. The part of this that really struck me was how much fun that dog was having! It never looked like work or drudgery! It was fun to stay in step with his human. And they played after completing the mission. Just like the dog in this scenario, we find such joy in depending on our One who not only wants relationship but empowers us to do anything He asks us to do!

Abiding isn't about learning lessons. Instead, it's an increasing dependence on God for all that we need as we acknowledge we do not have enough. It's not learning more patience—it's asking Him to be our patience. It's not conjuring up more strength—it's asking Him to be our strength. This is not a place to just try harder, but to change your source. Trying harder will not generate more when everything is already available to you! You just ask.

Day in My Life

"Our faith in Jesus transfers God's righteousness to us and he now declares us flawless in his eyes. This means we can now enjoy true and lasting peace with God, all because of what our Lord Jesus, the Anointed One, has done for us. Our faith guarantees us permanent access into this marvelous kindness that has given us a perfect relationship with God. What incredible joy bursts forth within us as we keep on celebrating our hope of experiencing God's glory! But that's not all! Even in times of trouble we have a joyful confidence, knowing that our pressures will develop in us patient endurance. And patient endurance will refine our character, and proven character leads us back to hope. And this hope is not a disappointing fantasy, because we can now experience the endless love of God cascading into our hearts through the Holy Spirit who lives in us!"

Romans 5:1–5

Breaking Free

I'd like to give you a little glimpse into a day in my life to help personalize the concept of abiding a bit more. I would also like you to hear me in my humble pronouncement that I do not have this figured out yet! I do acknowledge, though, that I am much happier and enjoy life when I am abiding.

So, I might wake up talking to Jesus (something that hasn't always been my habit but has become more common as He renews my mind and helps me focus on Him more) and roll out of bed. I plod downstairs in the dark to make coffee and read my Bible. I pretty quickly fall asleep while reading, and wake with a jerk to realize it's almost time to wake my son for school. And Jesus just says, *It's ok; come back to Me.*

Now, the kids are up and getting ready for school. Well, in theory, they are getting ready for school, and I have no patience as they get distracted with toys and anything else remotely interesting in the house. I stop and breathe—*Father, thank you that you are my patience today and that I don't have to drum up enough.*

I get a little snarky at my husband on the way out the door and feel guilty all the way to drop my kids off at school. I stop and breathe—*Father, I messed up. Thank You that You have already forgiven me*—and I call my husband to tell him I'm sorry.

Then I'm off to work, where I spend my day talking to people who are discouraged, defeated, and suffering. I start to take on all those feelings and drown a little. I stop and breathe—*Jesus, you are welcome here. You are the Counselor, not me, and You are at work in people's lives not just during the hour*

I meet with them, but all the rest of the day. I give You all the burdens I've received today; thank You for taking them because You know exactly what to do with them, and You relieve me.

Driving home, a car cuts me off, and I must slam on the brakes to avoid hitting them. Ahh!! I stop and breathe—*Thanks, Father, that You are even big enough for road rage, and I don't have to drive around angry the rest of the day because of that one person. I pray for them in whatever is going on in their lives.*

Four hours later, I realize I have been obsessing over being left out of plans for the weekend with friends. I have beaten up on myself the whole time, having gone from just being left out to having regurgitated all the ways I have failed, making me probably the worst person to walk the planet. This stings, but I realize it doesn't have to define me or my day. I stop and breathe—*Father, I'm so glad that You never leave me out and that You delight in me.*

I read the world news later that evening—war, sickness, and suffering. Discouragement creeps in thick and cold, making me feel as if I am going to ooze into the floor. How am I going to respond? Worst-case scenarios, worry, fear. I stop and breathe—*Remind me, tender Father, that You have all of this, and I don't need to take it on as my burden. I know You are working deep underground in all the chaos, and each moment draws me closer to you. Thank You that I will get to keep coming back to you alone for my fulfillment, peace, and hope. Thank You for hope, even in circumstances that seem to claim the opposite.*

Breaking Free

We are not seeking perfection, but dependence; not strength, but weakness; not success in the world's eyes, but belonging in God's; not condemnation, but freedom; not rules or a formula, but relationship.

We forget often, but God is faithful to keep calling us back to Himself. He wants us to remain in relationship with Him, to be our source for everything. If you want to know how to abide, ask and keep asking. He will not hide from you or your need.

Going Deeper:

1. What are some anchors God has given you personally to call you back to a place of connection with Him?

2. What situations or circumstances are more than you can handle for the day? (Spoiler alert: it's everything, but what are some you've seen today)? Ask Him to be what you need.

3. Are there places you need to erect a roadblock in your head to keep yourself from going down that path? Ask Jesus for the strength to do so.

4. Practice doing a brain dump with what is troubling you—recognizing you are not God, and you have a God.

Hannah Morrell

Who Is God?

> "But the great thing to remember is that, though our feelings come and go, [God's] love for us does not."
> —C.S. Lewis[15]

Someone once suggested that there should be a book about all the wrong done in the world in the name of God or Christianity, saying that such a book would help separate the real God from the mess evil people have created in His name. I think we often shy away from even being called Christians because of the implication that we are like "those" who have caused pain and agony to others in the name of God. We make many assumptions about God based on these past horrible evils, but also based on the suffering and grief in our own lives.

I would contrast our emotional and rational concepts of God, as Mike Wells did in his book *Sidetracked in the Wilderness*.[16] Our rational concepts of God are based upon what we have learned about Him through a variety of resources, including church gatherings, personal reading of the Bible, and the teachings of

---

15 Lewis, C.S. *Mere Christianity*. In *The Complete C. S. Lewis Signature Classics*. United Kingdom, HarperCollins, 2007.111.
16 Wells, Michael. *Sidetracked in the Wilderness: Find the Way Back to a Victorious Abundant Life*. United States, Devotional Life Press, 1999.

other believers. These might include descriptions like loving, holy, powerful, and tender.

Conversely, our emotional concepts of God are based on (mostly negative) experiences in our lives, often formed around a caricature of our pasts (father, mother, authority figure) or just the sum of our bad experiences. At the end of this chapter, I have included an emotional "God concept" test, the completion of which, I pray, will help you understand your honest emotional response to God. When our rational concept of God is that He is trustworthy, but our emotional concept is that He is not, we can understand why we feel conflicted when we think we must trust Him. Our minds might tell us that trusting Him is fine, but our emotions scream for us to run and protect ourselves.

When you take the emotional God concept test, there may be a temptation to pile on the guilt when you identify how you actually feel about God. I would urge you to reject this guilt, as I believe it is God's desire to show you the truth about Him. It is not your responsibility to fix the conflict, but to admit there is a possibility you may have an incorrect emotional concept. As you surrender this to God, He can change and revamp the whole thing. Guilt and shame about, however, will only drive you deeper into darkness. God does not use guilt and shame to manipulate us. He will show up in our pain and show us who He is, even when we are full of hatred towards Him because "Christ proved God's passionate love for us by dying in our place while we were still lost and ungodly!" (Romans 5:8).

I believe understanding the true character of God dramatically impacts our relationship with Him, and whether we will move into an abiding life of dependence on Him. If our emotional concept is quite skewed, He will not seem safe for relationship, and we want no part of depending on Him.

Who God is Not

Don't you know? Haven't you been listening? Yahweh is the one and only everlasting God, the Creator of all you can see and imagine! He never gets weary or worn out. His intelligence is unlimited; he is never puzzled over what to do! He empowers the feeble and infuses the powerless with increasing strength.
Isaiah 40:28–29

First, we must look at who God is not. These will most probably be the descriptions that surface because of your completing the God concept test. He is not:

- passive
- abusive
- unloving
- dismissive
- disappointed
- condemning
- tired of you
- irritable
- impatient
- shaming
- manipulative
- disconnected
- imposer of impossible standards
- punishing
- betraying
- abandoning

Let me walk you through how to discover this in the emotional concept test. If you answer the first question with something like, "you don't want to trust," "it's hopeless if you must trust," or "God won't actually do anything," these responses demonstrate you believe God is untrustworthy, unfaithful, or passive in His lack of response to your pain. If you are frustrated with God because He seems to just want to leave you to hurt or doesn't show up in the way you wanted Him to, you believe He is abusive or unloving. If you wish God would just kill you or change everything about you, you believe He is disappointed in you and, again, unloving. This continues throughout the questions, illustrating that what we believe in pain is what we truly believe.

> TRUST MAKES NO SENSE WHEN THE INDIVIDUAL TO BE TRUSTED IS NOT WORTHY OF TRUST.

You can see how in telling someone to trust God, if that person believes God is an awful jerk just waiting to punish them, the person wouldn't respond well! Or telling someone to wait on God, when they believe Him to be a passive, missing-in-action loser who won't bother to show up when they are hurting, would make them feel like reacting! Trust makes no sense when the individual to be trusted is not worthy of trust.

What Do You Do With The Emotional Concept?

> He understands humanity, for as a man, our magnificent King-Priest was tempted in every way just as we are, and conquered sin. So now we draw near freely and boldly to where grace is enthroned, to receive mercy's kiss and discover the grace we urgently need to strengthen us in our time of weakness.
> Hebrews 4:15–16

If God does not have the characteristics of our emotional concepts, but we still feel they are true, what do we do? We can't just convince your emotions that God really is good and you shouldn't feel this way.

Breaking Free

First, we must admit this is honestly how we feel. Emotional and rational concepts of God repel each other and make us feel divided. We must know where we are before we can know where we are going. I think for a lot of Christians, this becomes very difficult. Maybe we are afraid of being seen as what we really believe, or afraid of what we will have to face, but God already knows! Let's get real with Him and ourselves and stop pretending.

Philip Yancey's memoir, *Where the Light Fell,* is a very honest and painful portrayal of the religious community that raised Yancey, causing him to constantly feel like a disappointment and want to flee the faith entirely.[17] This community, and his mother specifically, promoted image above reality, leading her to demand perfection from Yancey and his brother, while not providing love. I am grateful that this pain has pushed Yancey to dive into many hard questions in the Christian faith rather than glossing over them or pretending they are not there. We must be honest before we can actually move from a place of image and suppression.

Second, we ask God to change this concept. Again, it's His job, not ours. He knows we need to be led to Truth, and as our Shepherd, He does this. He seeks the lost lambs (Matthew 18:10–14). He searches for the lost coins (Luke 15:8–10). He looks for the buried treasure (Matthew 13:44–46). He doesn't leave us where we are. In surrendering this emotional concept to Him and admitting what we really believe about Him, we are

---

[17] Yancey, Philip. *Where the Light Fell: A Memoir.* United States, Crown Publishing Group, 2021.

providing Him the opportunity to love us and move us into a different place.

Third, invite Jesus into the mess. Don't try to clean it up first. As we ask Him to change our God-concept, we have to allow Him to come in and sit down with us in the middle of it. The more we recognize our lack of strength, of faith, and of power, the more we can come in vulnerability to God for what we need. He doesn't want us to pretend we are fine. He wants the chance to be with us, even if that is right in the big middle of chaos we have created around ourselves. He walks right into the disaster and holds us close. He has been waiting for this chance the entire time, as His goal for us is relationship with Him (John 17:3).

The True Character of God

Jesus said to them, "I give you this eternal truth: I have existed long before Abraham was born, for I AM!"

John 8:58

If He is not the characteristics we've already listed, Who is He? What will He show us when we get honest and ask Him to change our concept of Him by revealing the Truth?

He is our loving Father and Love itself (1 John 4:8). Love is not something for which must perform; rather, love is something for us to settle into and enjoy. God's love is not dependent on what we do or how good we think we are.

Those who are loved by God, let his love continually pour from you to one another, because God is love. Everyone who loves is fathered

> by God and experiences an intimate knowledge of him. The one who doesn't love has yet to know God, for God is love.
>
> 1 John 4:7–8

> So I kneel humbly in awe before the Father of our Lord Jesus, the Messiah, the perfect Father of every father and child in heaven and on the earth. And I pray that he would unveil within you the unlimited riches of his glory and favor until supernatural strength floods your innermost being with his divine might and explosive power.
>
> Ephesians 3:14–16

> Love is large and incredibly patient. Love is gentle and consistently kind to all. It refuses to be jealous when blessing comes to someone else. Love does not brag about one's achievements nor inflate its own importance. Love does not traffic in shame and disrespect, nor selfishly seek its own honor. Love is not easily irritated or quick to take offense. Love joyfully celebrates honesty and finds no delight in what is wrong. Love is a safe place of shelter, for it never stops believing the best for others. Love never takes failure as defeat, for it never gives up.
>
> 1 Corinthians 13:4–7

He is not condemning, for He has taken all condemnation. This is the opposite of so much religious garbage in our world today. Judgement, condemnation, and brutal anger are everywhere as people beat up on each other with their words. Jesus took all the condemnation and sin to the cross with Him, so why would we negate His death and resurrection by bringing it up again?

> So now the case is closed. There remains no accusing voice of condemnation against those who are joined in life-union with Jesus, the Anointed One.
>
> Romans 8:1

He is good, a promise keeper, faithful, trustworthy, and ready to receive you. I know it doesn't always feel that way because we assume our comfort means our good. His definition of good often doesn't seem to include our comfort. But that doesn't negate the good. He knows what ultimately is good for us and loves us enough to be with us through all of it.

Our good is not always what we would wish it to be. His goal is not that you've made it through life with no suffering. Instead, His goal is that you know Him. In John 17:3, He actually defines Eternal Life as knowing Him. So, our good is knowing Him. This is where Life is found.

> *For Yahweh is always good and ready to receive you. He's so loving that it will amaze you—so kind that it will astound you! And He is famous for His faithfulness toward all. Everyone knows our God can be trusted, for he keeps his promises to every generation!*
> Psalms 100:5

> *You are the Lord who reigns over your never-ending kingdom through all the ages of time and eternity! You are faithful to fulfill every promise you've made. You manifest yourself as kindness in all you do. Weak and feeble ones you will sustain. Those bent over with burdens of shame you will lift up. You have captured our attention and the eyes of all look to you. You give what they hunger for at just the right time. When you open your generous hand, it's full of blessings, satisfying the longings of every living thing. You are fair and righteous in everything you do, and your love is wrapped into all your works. You draw near to those who call out to you, listening closely, especially when their hearts are true. Every godly one receives even more than what they ask for. For you hear what their hearts really long for, and you bring them your saving strength.*
> Psalms 145:13–19

> *So we are convinced that every detail of our lives is continually woven together for good, for we are his lovers who have been called to fulfill his designed purpose.*
> Romans 8:28

He is emotionally connected and approachable. He is our comforter in sorrow. When my son was six months old, he had a severe allergic reaction to something, and we had to pursue testing to figure out what solid foods would not kill him. The allergist we saw was very kind, but as a new mom with a tiny baby, it was hard to willingly present my baby to be poked and prodded.

I held him close and cried as I watched him writhe in frustration while the welts from the scratch tests grew enormous, and my hope for a quick and easy solution to this problem diminished greatly. The nurses attempted to get blood for the blood test that would follow from both his wrists and his feet. His little veins were not providing enough from any of the sites. I wept through this as my son screamed. Medical staff eventually said they would have to try again in a few months because even with all the pain, they had not gathered enough blood. His little eyes kept looking at me as if to ask why on earth I could bring him to be tortured.

God reminded me that, just as I didn't leave my son and go get coffee while he was suffering, neither is He absent in pain. He weeps with us as our pain goes to His heart, because we are His beloved children. If I, as a human mom who tries her best but fails often, would never abandon my son amid suffering, how much more would He stand with us and hold us as we ache? He showed me that often He can't explain why the pain is necessary, just as I couldn't explain it to my baby and have it make sense. But that didn't mean He would ever abandon us in it. And even when we look at Him as if He has betrayed us and brought us to suffering for no reason, He stays with us and holds us close.

Jesus stands with us and understands the pain. He is a high priest who is not distant or absent but has experienced the suffering (Hebrews 4:15). He loves us so much and weeps with us as we mourn. He is not untouched by our suffering or waiting until we get our act together but kneels down with us in the mess and holds us close. Remember that a single circumstance doesn't define the character of God—He is the same yesterday, today and forever (Hebrews 13:8). And His love is overflowing, compassionate and personal. He will not abandon us in suffering, but waits with steadfastness and holds us through everything.

> *When they [Israel] suffered, he suffered with them. The Angel of His Presence saved them. Out of his enduring love and compassion he redeemed them. He lifted them up, carried them in his arms, and cared for them all the days of old.*
>
> Isaiah 63:9

> *So then, we must cling in faith to all we know to be true. For we have a magnificent King-Priest, Jesus Christ, the Son of God, who rose into the heavenly realm for us, and now sympathizes with us in our frailty. He understands humanity, for as a man, our magnificent King-Priest was tempted in every way just as we are, and conquered sin. So now we draw near freely and boldly to where grace is enthroned, to receive mercy's kiss and discover the grace we urgently need to strengthen us in our time of weakness.*
>
> Hebrews 4:14–16

He is the Provider, although He does not always provide in the way we expect, or "plan" for Him to. When we bought our first house, we developed a list of things that needed to be done to it, but we lacked the money to do them. They were fairly important items like replacing the water heater, removing a rusted tub, and that sort of thing, but after making the list, I promptly put it in a drawer because I had no hope of completing any of the list for a long time. A year later, I found that list, and everything on it had been done. I was making almost no money, and my husband had not received a windfall. There really was no explanation for it being done other than God had made it happen.

> Jesus said to them, "I am the Bread of Life. Come every day to me and you will never be hungry. Believe in me and you will never be thirsty."
> John 6:35

> I am convinced that my God will fully satisfy every need you have, for I have seen the abundant riches of glory revealed to me through Jesus Christ!
> Philippians 4:19

He is the Empowerer. This means you don't have to be afraid of weakness or lack. You can celebrate your weakness as it becomes a portal for God's power within you (2 Corinthians 12:9–10). He doesn't just have power for Himself. He provides everything we need for life each day. He is faithful to be enough for the moment, regardless of how hopeless it might seem. We get to enjoy His power and strength rather than getting hung up on our lack of both.

> I know what it means to lack, and I know what it means to experience overwhelming abundance. For I'm trained in the secret of overcoming all things, whether in fullness or in hunger. And I find that the strength of Christ's explosive power infuses me to conquer every difficulty.
> Philippians 4:12–13

He is a safe place, a wraparound shield. There are very few safe places in today's world. We don't often feel we can just be ourselves; instead, we more often feel the need to maintain an image or a performance or blatantly live in lies to keep ourselves "safe." He is a place for us to rest, to let go of the performance, and to just retreat into His presence.

> *You're my place of quiet retreat, and your wraparound presence becomes my shield as I wrap myself in your Word!*
> *Psalms 119:114*

He is faithful, even when we are not. His faithfulness is not dependent on our holding up an end of the bargain. He responds in love to us regardless of our behavior, reminding us we would be much happier if we would allow Him to move us in His direction, but meanwhile, His love and faithfulness will never change.

> *Yahweh's tender mercies have no end, and the kindness of his endless love is never exhausted. New, fresh mercies greet me with every sunrise. So wonderfully great is your faithfulness!*
> *Lamentations 3:22–23*

He is merciful, not holding our wrongs up to us and punishing us for them. He meets us with kindness and compassion, grace upon grace. There is no limit to the mercy He extends to us. My mercy is a sad, pathetic excuse in comparison to His. Corrie ten Boom said that He takes our sins and throws them into the deepest lake and puts up a sign that says, "No Fishing." This is mercy! He chooses to remember our sin no more (Jeremiah 31:34). When He looks at us, He does not see our failures. He sees our being made perfect in Jesus.

> *For my thoughts about mercy are not like your thoughts, and my ways are different from yours. As high as the heavens are above the earth, so my ways and my thoughts are higher than yours.*
> *Isaiah 55:8–9*

The translator's footnote in the Passion Translation says, "In the context, the thoughts of God are in reference to compassion, mercy, and forgiveness. Man's thoughts of mercy are not God's.

Man's mercy runs out, but God's mercy is higher than the heavens. God's mercy and forgiveness are generous and abundant."

Revelation as a Process

For if you embrace the truth, it will release true freedom into your lives.
John 8:32

Now, don't be worried if you haven't bought into some of this yet. I think that believing this requires a revelation from God Himself. Revelation is like birth—it can't be rushed, and the process is painful and totally worthwhile in the end. His goal in life is that we know Him, so it is pretty important to Him that we get this revelation. However, He knows we cannot handle it all at once. He waits until we are ready. I know sometimes we think we want to rush through and get it all at once. But He knows what we are ready for, and He works in those specific places in order to reveal who He is in them.

As you go through the list of characteristics of God listed above (which is not exhaustive, by the way, but just a start), ask how these apply to you personally. How are You my safe place, God? How are You providing for me? How are You loving me? We really need this to be individual and applicable to our lives rather than just a nice concept. I believe He will be faithful to bring these things into focus in your life as you learn how He already IS this way to you. This revelation allows you

> ABIDING LIFE DEPENDS ON TRUSTING THE VINE TO PROVIDE ALL WE NEED AND BELIEVING HE IS WHO HE SAYS HE IS.

to move into a relationship with Him that isn't possible if you believe lies about Him or if you are waiting for Him to be awful to you. Abiding life depends on trusting the Vine to provide all we need and believing He is Who He says He is. Only in this relationship will we relax into allowing Him to provide all we need for this life.

Going Deeper:

1. Take the God concept test below and discover how it helps identify your emotional concept of God.

    a. When you are in the middle of a terrible day and think about trusting God, what do you feel?
    b. What frustrates you about God when all circumstances seem against you?
    c. What do you wish God would do in your life?
    d. When, if ever, does God surprise you?
    e. When, if ever, do you enjoy God?
    f. What things about yourself are you convinced you must change for God to love or even accept you?
    g. How do you think God feels about you?
    h. What are you afraid God will do to you if you continue as you are today?
    i. What do you think God wants from you?
    j. When, if ever, can you depend on God?

2. Come to Him admitting what you feel (and thus believe) about Him. Recognize that those feelings make you divided and also normal!

3. Meditate on some of these characteristics we've talked about above, asking God how they apply personally to you and how He will show you who He really is.

Hannah Morrell

What Does God Want From Us?

"Do you realize that it is only in the gospel of Jesus Christ that you get the verdict before the performance?"

—Tim Keller[18]

What does God want from us if He is not the mean ogre we have made Him out to be? If His character differs greatly from the emotional concept of Him we have maintained, what is His desire in relationship with us? So often we impose incredibly tough standards on ourselves, thinking that by meeting them, we will maintain our relationship with God. We believe Him to be waiting for us to mess up so He can ditch us.

Have you ever considered all He does to maintain relationship with us? He holds us together, stays close, comforts in every circumstance (even the ones we have brought on ourselves), empowers us, woos us, loves us, has patience with us, and never stops pursuing us. Instead of acknowledging this, though, we obsess on whether we have read the Bible regularly, attended a suitable number of church services, or tried not to screw up too much. We often make relationship with God, or

---

18 Keller, Timothy. *The Freedom of Self-forgetfulness: The Path to True Christian Joy.* United Kingdom, 10Publishing, 2012.

abiding life, very complicated and completely up to our own strength and behavior.

What God Doesn't Want From Us

For by grace you have been saved by faith. Nothing you did could ever earn this salvation, for it was the love gift from God that brought us to Christ! So no one will ever be able to boast, for salvation is never a reward for good works or human striving.
Ephesians 2:8–9

Why don't we start with what God doesn't want from us? First, He doesn't require us to be anyone's savior. (That includes being our own savior, by the way.) I used to think it was my job to save those in my life whom I loved, and the requirement was being a "perfect witness," or it wouldn't work. I remember distinctly the day God told me I was not supposed to save anyone—He had already done all that work. I haven't saved myself or anyone else. I have trusted God to save me and to save those whom I love.

We can never know where, when, or how anyone will come to know God. I used to scheme about certain books or people or videos that would surely be the impetus for someone to want to know Jesus. But I know now that I could never draw close to even guessing what it will be that initiates that desire.

When my brother finally admitted he was an alcoholic, he did so during an interaction with a complete stranger after years of my family's pursuing him to get help. None of my pressure or complaints led to this change, and how it came to be a stranger who prompted the admission we will never know. But my brother has remained sober ever since and has worked extremely hard to recover from the physical, emotional, and spiritual ramifications of the addiction. His experience has taught me many things, one of which is that we have no clue how God will get someone's attention.

We cannot control or manipulate revelation in anyone. Only God gives revelation, and He knows exactly the way to do it for each person. When I take responsibility on myself for someone else's salvation, I am trying to do God's job, and I am a terrible god.

Second, He doesn't want us trying to meet His standard through the law. He literally made it impossible to be perfect without Him. We can try, but we can't achieve the perfection He requests in Matthew 5:48. Why? Because our godliness is only possible with His Life within us.

The commandments given in Scripture become promises when we realize they are only possible through the Life He has given us in Jesus. Instead of trying to gather enough strength to perform adequately, what if you admitted you couldn't live the Christian life on your own and asked Him to live through you? He is already perfect and meets God's standard through us. He is already loving, so love for even the most unlovable is possible. And this is not because we have worked really hard to grit it out. We get to rest internally from the struggle and let Him be all that He is through us.

God does not ask or expect us to obsess about sin or focus on the flesh to keep from sinning. I remember sitting in my first chapel service at my brand-new college, where we were all given a piece of paper with several questions on it. We were then instructed to analyze ourselves to identify all kinds of sins and confess them. I moved into enormous condemnation over this exercise.

> THE COMMANDMENTS GIVEN IN SCRIPTURE BECOMES PROMISES WHEN WE REALIZE THEY ARE ONLY POSSIBLE THROUGH THE LIFE HE HAS GIVEN US IN JESUS.

Overwhelmed by guilt, I felt as though I was failing in all areas of my life. What the staff forgot to mention in this chapel session was that Jesus had already dealt with sin on the cross, so our sin no longer owned or controlled us! We were not going to crucify Jesus over and over again every time we sinned. At the cross, He took all the sin—past, present, and future—on Himself to free us from its slavery. If I get obsessive about sin and wear condemnation for it, I am basically saying that Jesus' sacrifice and blood were not enough, and I need to really give in to guilt (to whatever degree I decide) in order to get through it.

I think we do this because we feel if we pummel ourselves enough, we won't sin again. I don't find this to be helpful, as the obsession just makes me focus even more on the sin. As I mentioned in chapter 5, mental flagellation fixes nothing. Instead, when Jesus becomes our focus, His power causes sin to lose any power it suggests it may have over us.

Finally, God does not want us to believe that more information is going to fix things. We tend to get obsessive with knowledge, and, as we've already addressed, knowledge without power will not achieve what we hope it will (John 5:39–40).

I do believe it is great to study the Bible and increase your knowledge about God—but the appetite for knowledge must balance with actually knowing God; we also must acknowledge that information alone will not bring about relationship. He so greatly desires relationship, and we miss so much when we make it simply about more knowledge. We are to worship God in spirit and in truth (John 4:24). Truth alone makes us dry and stuck in our heads, and spirit alone makes us volatile and undiscerning. The combination is just right.

When we realize what God does not want from us, we can more clearly see His foundation for relationship with us is really His responsibility. He has pursued relationship with us and will continue to do so, wanting more than anything for us to rest in our connection to the Vine as a branch.

What God Wants From Us

> Now this is what Yahweh says: "Listen, Jacob, to the One who created you, Israel, to the one who shaped who you are. Do not fear, for I, your Kinsman-Redeemer, will rescue you. I have called you by name, and you are mine."
>
> Isaiah 43:1

What does God want from us, then? First, He wants us to recognize our belonging. All of us want to know we belong, that we are accepted. That's why rejection hurts so much. But everything from the beginning of time until now is God saying, "I want you; I desire you. Be with me; you belong to me. I will never forsake you; you are mine." This is what God's love means—it's not just His tolerance of us, putting up with us because He feels He must. We have cheapened it and made it love based on what we do or do not do. Our behavior does not limit love. God's love thrums a steady rhythm—*I love you; I love you; I love you.* "But," we protest, "I did this bad thing!" *I love you.* "But I can't get it right!" *I love you.* "But I can't do enough!" *I love you.*

God is constantly offering the belonging, but we must accept it to enjoy it. We must embrace our identity as helpless to save ourselves and also as completely and utterly loved and made new.

In reading *The Water Keeper* by Charles Martin, the following amazing paragraph about belonging stuck with me. The book is fiction, but it does a great job of bringing truth through the stories of fictional people. The main character of the book rescues people from trafficking and thinks:

> *Who am I? And more importantly, whose am I? In my life, in my strange line of work, I'd discovered that we as people can't answer the first until someone else answers the second. It's a function of design. Belonging comes before identity. Ownership births purpose. Someone speaks whose we are, and out of that we become who we are. It's just the way the heart works. In Eden, we walked in the cool of the evening with a Father who, by the very nature of the conversations and time spent together, answered our heart's cry. It was the product of relationship. But out here, somewhere east or west of the Garden, beyond the shadow of the fiery walls, we have trouble hearing what He's saying. And even when we do, we have trouble believing Him. So we wrestle and search. But regardless of where we search and how we try to answer the question or what we ingest, inject, or swallow the numb the nagging, only the Father gets to tell us who we are. Period.*[19]

---

[19] Martin, Charles. *The Water Keeper.* United States, Thomas Nelson, 2020. 183.

Breaking Free

Second, we get to recognize we can't do it on our own! What do I mean by "it"? Anything and everything! We can't live the Christian life. We can't figure out the formula for life. We can't gain success in God's eyes. We were never supposed to do all this on our own. God has created us for dependence on Him.

> *I am the sprouting vine and you're my branches. As you live in union with me as your source, fruitfulness will stream from within you—but when you live separated from me you are powerless.*
> *John 15:5*

Congratulations! You nailed the standard! You can do nothing apart from Jesus. So, if you've achieved nothing, you have met God's standard. Quit trying to do something without the power to achieve it.

The really good news is that Christ died to eliminate our sin, but He also lives within us so that we can do Life. You have all you need for Life in Him, and He is willing and able to give it to you. We must remain attached to Him as a branch on the Vine for this to be possible. Obedience, then, results from His work and His Life flowing from Him—the Vine—through us, the branch. Obedience is not the catalyst for relationship with God, but rather the natural outpouring of that relationship. We get the order wrong, and we end up discouraged and drained.

> *For he is the complete fullness of deity living in human form. And our own completeness is now found in him. We are completely filled with God as Christ's fullness overflows within us. He is the Head of every kingdom and authority in the universe!*
> *Colossians 2:9–10*

All of God is in Christ, and all of Christ is in us, as one of my old Bible teachers used to say. We lack nothing.

To make it even better, we are co-seated with Him in the heavenlies already (Ephesians 2:6). How does that work? I can't wrap my brain around it, but it's also hard to understand how I already died with Christ and live His Life now (Galatians 2:20). If I live from my place of already having victory, I can rise above any circumstance in my life and see it from a different perspective.

> *He raised us up with Christ the exalted One, and we ascended with him into the glorious perfection and authority of the heavenly realm, for we are now co-seated as one with Christ!*
> *Ephesians 2:6*

We have the power we need for any and every problem through Him. We don't have to create a solution; rather, we recognize He is the solution indwelling us and is ready for action. Whenever you see you are lacking or weak, admit it, and just ask Him to be all that you need! His miraculous power provides energy, strength, patience, wisdom—all of it!

> *Never doubt God's mighty power to work in you and accomplish all this. He will achieve infinitely more than your greatest request, your most unbelievable dream, and your wildest imagination! He will outdo them all, for his miraculous power constantly energizes you.*
> *Ephesians 3:20*

One of the greatest lessons my friend and mentor, Mike Wells, taught me was that I wasn't just to show up with whatever I had generated and hope it was enough for the situation in front of me. Instead, I was simply to come with an empty bag and ask Jesus to fill it. When I first started counseling, God brought me the weirdest problems—issues that my seminary classes had never addressed. I was overwhelmed. I had no idea what to do or say to these people. I burned out and quit because I thought I was supposed to have what it took to "fix" these people.

This second time around, whenever I meet someone, I begin by admitting I don't have a clue about what this person needs and ask Jesus to fill my empty bag with what will be helpful for them. I am often surprised by the things that come out of my mouth because, as I submit to Him and ask Him to be my words, He says really cool things! I get to be a part of that. All I have to do is ask.

> Ask, and the gift is yours. Seek, and you'll discover. Knock, and the door will be opened for you.
>
> Matthew 7:7

Finally, we are created for rest! When we learn that the Christian life is all about rest rather than effort, it is such a relief! Commandments become promises, for He will achieve these through you as you remain dependent on Him. Weakness is a portal for strength, not a source of embarrassment or hiding.

Abiding life allows us to rest and enjoy the journey, not putting impossible standards on ourselves from our own resources. With God's power as the source, we can do the impossible and live in joy and peace. Relationship with Him provides all we need without the burden of trying to perform to earn or maintain His love.

> ABIDING LIFE ALLOWS US TO REST AND ENJOY THE JOURNEY.

How Do We Depend and Rest?

> We look away from the natural realm and we focus our attention and expectation onto Jesus who birthed faith within us and who leads us forward into faith's perfection. His example is this: Because his heart was focused on the joy of knowing that you would be his, he endured the agony of the cross and conquered its humiliation, and now sits exalted at the right hand of the throne of God!
>
> Hebrews 12:2

In learning to depend on Him and experience rest in the Christian life, I believe focus is preeminent. Whatever gets your focus owns you. So, if we focus on Him when we feel weak, we are allowing Him to live through us. If we focus on Him when we feel like a failure, we will see Him achieve success (His version of it, not the world's) through us. If we focus on Him when we feel unloved, we will be bathed in the deepest love we have ever experienced.

> Yes, feast on all the treasures of the heavenly realm and fill your thoughts with heavenly realities, and not with the distractions of the natural realm.
>
> Colossians 3:2

> Don't be pulled in different directions or worried about a thing. Be saturated in prayer throughout each day, offering your faith-filled requests before God with overflowing gratitude. Tell him every detail of your life, then God's wonderful peace that transcends human understanding, will guard your heart and mind through Jesus Christ. Keep your thoughts continually fixed on all that is authentic and real, honorable and admirable, beautiful and respectful, pure and holy, merciful and kind. And fasten your thoughts on every glorious work of God, praising him always.
>
> Philippians 4:6–8

The Bible has a lot to say about where we focus. Don't be afraid to ask God for a changed focus. When we focus on Jesus, our problems don't go away, but perspective shifts dramatically. It doesn't feel as though our problems are the only thing in front of us. We see our Jesus has power to deal with them for us.

Focus-shifting is often helpful in difficult circumstances, as we acknowledge we have a God, and He is at work. I know He generally does not work in the way we would expect, but He is always loving us through it. I use all sorts of reminders to bring me back to a changed focus. Anchors (physical representations of the intangible) are helpful sometimes, like a bracelet you wear, a point in the road that reminds you, or a flower popping up in a place you didn't expect. I have realized that even my clumsiness is a call back to focusing on Jesus, and now I no longer get so frustrated when I get stuck or trip over something. I also like to set up mental altars for all the ways God has been active in my life so that I can remind myself when it feels as if He is far away. Anything that helps us to refocus is helpful for our rising above the physical circumstance to see past it to the spiritual Truth of His Life in you as He brings all the power you need for it.

So, to revisit what God wants from us, I would sum it up like this:

- Admit your lack and be still
- Accept and recognize His Life within, turning to Him for every need
- Rest
- Refocus

This may sound wrong for a long while because when we have heard the wrong thing for so long, the right thing may sound ridiculous. Religion ends at my feet, where I must produce fruit, create good works, and satisfy God with my behavior. Faith in Christ ends at God's feet, and He must produce, create, and satisfy His requirements through us.

I love the contrast Tim Keller makes between obedience from love instead of obedience from trying to get something from God:

> *In religion, you obey because God is useful. In Christianity, you obey because God is beautiful.*[20]

We can't go from the love which brought you to salvation through relationship with Jesus to the legalism of trying to do more, be more, get it right, and don't mess it up. It is always love. It is always relationship. The one thing God wants from you is to enjoy relationship with Him. Everything else results from this, a natural outflow of looking to Him for all we need.

---

20 Keller, Timothy [@timkellernyc]. "In religion, you obey because God is useful. In Christianity, you obey because God is beautiful." Twitter, February 18, 2019, https://twitter.com/timkellernyc/status/1097468524363157504.

Breaking Free
Going Deeper:

1. Soak in the belonging. Admit your lack—whatever you don't have for the day, tell Him. Ask Him to show you how He meets your need.

2. What would be different about your day and life if rest were your priority? What would motivate your work rather than busyness?

3. How do you refocus when you are distracted? Ask Him to focus you.

4. How does love fulfill the commandments through you?

Hannah Morrell

What Do We Do With People?

"I am the prodigal son every time I search for unconditional love where it cannot be found."
—Henri Nouwen[21]

As I have been saying throughout this book, we are created for relationship. We are made for relationship with God and also with people. He is three-in-one, the Trinity. The Father, Son, and Spirit all have relationship together and generate the relationship with us out of their own love and unity. We get to have this communion with other people as well, but often this can be rather messy.

When I talk about the Church, I will use a capital letter because I believe the Church is one—the bride of Christ. There are not a number of different churches, but rather a number of clubs that are organized out of the true Church. So, what is the Church supposed to be?

Paul talks about the Church quite a lot, and I would define it as the community of believers in Jesus who together are the hands and feet of God in the world. They are the demonstrators

---

[21] Nouwen, Henri J. M. *The Return of the Prodigal Son*. United Kingdom, Darton, Longman and Todd, 1992. 43

of the relationship God has with us—the visible presence of His love and Life in a world that is hurting.

> *But some of our body parts don't require as much attention. Instead, God has mingled the body parts together, giving greater honor to the "lesser" members who lacked it. He has done this intentionally so that every member would look after the others with mutual concern, and so that there will be no division in the body. In that way, whatever happens to one member happens to all. If one suffers, everyone suffers. If one is honored, everyone rejoices. You are the body of the Anointed One, and each of you is a unique and vital part of it.*
> 1 Corinthians 12:24–27

The Church is intended to be a body of people who care for each other and for outsiders with love, grace, and discernment. We are to be known by our love. This means that, by definition, the Church should practice incredible love for others, whether or not they are a part of the body.

This body of believers, however, is also made up of broken people in process, people who still struggle with many issues, who still mess up in loving, who still hurt each other and condemn in fear sometimes. So, how do we function in such a crazy group of people?

Get The Order Right

> *Our love for others is our grateful response to the love God first demonstrated to us.*
> 1 John 4:19

First, I think we need to get our order right with human relationships. If I give you my phone number, telling you can call me anytime you want, and then proceed to tell you there are three 2's, a 3, a 5, a 6, two 7's and an 8, you can't actually call me! You need an order. We often get the order wrong regarding relationships with people, which results in our inability to put things in perspective or maintain healthy relationships. We need to allow God's relationship with us to satisfy basic needs first, and then human relationships can fall in the proper order.

Human relationships are not supposed to meet the needs only God can satisfy, but they are often the first place we go in looking for love, acceptance, purpose, and belonging. Human relationships can satisfy none of these needs. We try, but something always happens (whether real or inferred) which makes us feel unloved, unacceptable, without purpose, or rejected. People can become our idols when we try to worship at their feet to earn love and acceptance from them. And all that worshipping doesn't give us the desired result. I believe it is impossible for a person to meet these needs, no matter how hard we try to make them do so.

In relationships, idolatry can look like an intense need for a particular relationship to work in your life, and so you do as you must to find your worth in their eyes. Or it may reveal itself as the opposite, when someone in your past who hurt you still controls your very being. In this second case, it is like writing a blank check to the one who abused, manipulated, or rejected you, allowing them to spend your life as they choose. These are never the people I would like to see in charge of your life.

> PEOPLE CAN BECOME OUR IDOLS WHEN WE TRY TO WORSHIP AT THEIR FEET TO EARN LOVE AND ACCEPTANCE FROM THEM.

Only in abiding in Christ, enjoying the relationship we have with God, can we find a firm foundation for our worth, acceptance, and love. If we try to put a person in the role of fulfilling this for us, we end up frustrated, disappointed, and rejected.

People Are Messy

But instead be kind and affectionate toward one another. Has God graciously forgiven you? Then graciously forgive one another in the depths of Christ's love.
Ephesians 4:32

Another problem with relating to people is that we expect relationships not to be messy. We are offended when others do something wrong and hurt us. We expect them to love us unconditionally, never messing up or lashing out when they feel rejected themselves. Of course, we can't meet these expectations ourselves, so we certainly cannot expect others to meet them for us either. I find it interesting that there are a lot of verses about forgiving others in the Bible, yet we expect to have people behave in such a way that they never need forgiveness.

The more I talk to people, the more I realize how crazy we all are. The expectations we often have for each other are those that God alone can meet. So when people "do us wrong," we become frustrated. When I expect someone to understand my perspective and they don't, I get offended and feel rejected and hurt. Why would they be able to read my mind? Or understand what's going on in my heart? People cannot meet expectations of unconditional love, constant acceptance, intentional purpose, or unquestioned belonging.

I spoke with a woman recently who told me she would finally feel rest and peace when everyone was happy with her. Gently, I reminded her that this was never a point she would reach, and she had to determine that rest and peace were possible only from her relationship with Jesus, not when people decided she was acceptable. If you are waiting for a similar situation, please know that I do not believe it is realistic or obtainable. And you will spend your life trying to control something you can't. We cannot try to live to everyone else's expectations, or we would run from one person to another, trying desperately to achieve standards we cannot maintain, or sometimes even meet.

I would also suggest that loving others from the love of God allows us to approach people when they are messy and disappointing, not trying to fix them but loving them right where they are. This is the love God gives us for others as we abide in relationship with Him.

Prepare to Be Offended

Love does not traffic in shame and disrespect, nor selfishly seek its own honor. Love is not easily irritated or quick to take offense.
1 Corinthians 13:5

Another expectation with relationships is that if they are "good" ones, we will never feel offended. My friend Mike Wells used to say that we must be willing to be offended until we can't be offended anymore.[22] This doesn't sound like a fun prospect, does it? If we choose to be controlled by every offense that comes from others, then we will withdraw, isolate, and shut down. Any real relationship would then be lacking, as we either posture to maintain an image that won't bring offense from someone or hide out and have no relationship at all.

Offense is not the worst thing to happen in relationship, as it challenges us to bring the issue to God to see if change is needed or ushers us into praying for the person who has offended us. I think this brings to light another issue—just because God reveals something in someone else that needs to be changed doesn't mean we are supposed to fix it or even bring it to their attention. Sometimes He will call us to address it, but more often, I believe, we our observations are a call to pray and leave it with God to sort out.

People Bring Suffering

He was despised and rejected by men, a man of deep sorrows who was no stranger to suffering and grief.
Isaiah 53:3

Finally, we incorrectly assume people will never be a part of the suffering that God promises will be ours in this world (John 16:33). We expect relationships to bring acceptance and love. Some of the deepest suffering people endure is from relationship—rejection, abandonment, betrayal, death, and loss.

---

22 Wells, Michael. "Fundamentals of the Abiding Life: Session #4." *Basic Seminar DVD Study Notes.* Abiding Life Ministries International. 19. https://abidinglife.com/pages/freeresources

Breaking Free

When we experience pain in one relationship, the automatic reaction for many is to avoid all relationships, hoping to ease the pain. But isolating doesn't make the pain go away. Suffering is a part of our life on this earth, and God promises to be with us through it all. After all, He knows rejection in a deeper way than we ever will. Jesus experienced rejection constantly while walking the earth and suffered much at the hands of people. He is compassionate and loving to us through the struggle and strengthens us to keep going back to relationship even when it has previously hurt us. We must realize that, in relationship, there is often pain, sometimes caused by others, that is difficult and may make us want to hide from people, but this is not what God calls us to.

Again, a small sidenote: I am not suggesting anyone should stay in an abusive relationship because there is purpose in suffering. I do believe God may sometimes call us to endure suffering, but that is always a clear call. If the motivation for relationship is fear, manipulation, or abuse, I do not advocate staying in that relationship.)

How Do We Cope With Pain in Relationships?

Adam answered, "I heard your powerful presence moving in the garden, and I was afraid because I was naked; so I hid."
Genesis 3:10

When we experience pain in relationship, how do we cope? I believe there are several personas we adopt in trying to deal with relationship problems. These personas are part of the flesh pattern we discussed in chapter three and are images we create to hide our pain. I do not believe they work in freeing us from our identity messages; instead, these personas compound and create more negative messages in our minds.

The first is the **pretender**. Pretenders posture that they have it all together, that people don't affect them one way or the other, and that they really don't need relationships. There is a sense of indifference when it comes to people, for they never want to be seen as needing or desiring relationship. These people create an image for themselves and then hide behind it. Anyone who tries to see behind the image is immediately expelled from the pretender's life so that the image can be maintained. They fear exposure.

Another persona is the **clown**, a person who has coped with rejection by becoming the funniest, most entertaining person around. I find it interesting to look at the lives of professional comedians, many of whom suffered incredible rejection and have learned to cope using humor. This is another form of hiding behind a self-protective wall which allows them to entertain and even make a living!

The **isolator** is, in some ways, the most obvious in terms of the way they deal with rejection. Because they have felt pain, they refuse relationship and become unable to receive love because it is too scary. The withdrawal eliminates the possibility of being rejected again, as they feel they are protecting themselves by complete relationship abstinence. These people believe they are islands with no need or desire for community or human connection. They may not be entirely without relationship (some are even married or have kids or friends) but are mentally and emotionally withdrawn from the relationships they do have. They are unwilling to become vulnerable or put themselves in any position that would require real communication, even while they are starving for healthy relationship.

Another way to cope with relationship problems is to settle. The **settler** has given up on having healthy and encouraging relationships and simply expects the pain to continue. They do have relationships of some kind, but they are not fulfilling or connected ones. Somewhere along the way, they have decided to just deal with it. These settlers won't really look for better relationships, but neither will they feel safe in the ones they have. Sometimes the settler can depend on unhealthy relationships, as they really don't know to function without a person rejecting them or without someone to help. This person generally doesn't know what to do without another person needing them, even if they are simply a punching bag for an abuser.

The **fighter** copes with rejection by rejecting before they can be rejected. It is like isolating but is more overt. Instead of just avoiding relationships altogether, the fighter pushes into conflict and sometimes creates it to justify keeping people at a distance. They don't have to focus on their own rejection because they are blaming someone else for their problems. Often, I find these people struggle with road rage, as they are convinced that their rage is changing wrong behavior in another driver while refusing to acknowledge their own behavior.

When the **clinger** experiences relationship pain, they will try to find acceptance everywhere and in any way possible. Because of this, they often smother those around them. Relationships with clingers are high maintenance, as they require constant input, without which, the clinger will pout and throw a tantrum. The clinger has learned that if they try to pile all their needs on a person, this individual will try their hardest to meet them. This isn't genuine acceptance, but they feel even a phony substitute is better than nothing. The demand for acceptance doesn't decrease in the presence of committed relationships, as clingers just move deeper and deeper into the obsession of getting everything they need out of one relationship. These people define themselves completely by others' perceptions, or at least by their assumption of those perceptions. They will contort themselves to be whatever they think another person wants, often losing who they want to be or who they are.

The **over-worker** deals with rejection by working harder, hoping that will make them more acceptable. This person often has a more task-related focus than relationship-related. They see acceptance as coming through getting everything right and being perfect. They are quick to recommit to being more diligent and driven in order to prevent rejection.

None of these personas help us have healthy relationships with people, and often we try to relate to God through them as well. We hide from people and God behind an image because we are hoping it will prevent pain. I don't believe this works, though, as we still end up experiencing pain, just alone, separate from relationship by our own choosing.

Breaking Free
How Do We Do It Differently?

While Jesus was at the Passover Feast, the number of his followers began to grow, and many gave their allegiance to him because of all the miraculous signs they had seen him doing! But Jesus did not yet entrust himself to them, because he knew how fickle human hearts can be. He needed no one to tell him about human nature, for he fully understood what man was capable of doing.

John 2:23–25

How do we change the way we've been coping with human rejection? We bring it to Jesus and let Him fix it. So often it feels as if our potential for relationship with people has been broken, either by others or by our own doing. We are comfortably uncomfortable with how we have allowed ourselves to deal with life, and the thought of changing brings a fear of vulnerability. But, if our needs for love and acceptance are first met by the One who loves us faithfully (regardless of our performance or lack thereof), then I would suggest we can approach human relationships differently.

Jesus's life on the earth demonstrated how to abide with God and have relationships with people. Jesus was constantly with people, but John 2:24 says He didn't entrust Himself to them. I would define this as not letting their praise or criticism define Him. Jesus had a firm foundation regardless of rejection or acceptance, which was good considering how changeable and inconsistent people showed themselves to be in His life. One minute He was the hero, and the next they were abandoning or criticizing Him.

I know this kind of relationship sounds impossible for us. And it is unless we go deeper to the root of His love and the acceptance that grounds us. If our basic needs are met in Him, we can approach human relationship for pleasure rather than need. This doesn't mean won't experience the pain of rejection or abandonment, but those feelings don't have to gut us completely because we stand on the foundation of complete love and acceptance in Christ.

Just like we need to get an order for the numbers in a phone number to place a call, we need to get the order right in relationships. God's relationship with us has to come first. We belong to Him first. He gives us life first. When we know He loves and accepts us and therefore don't depend on relationships with people to make us feel loved and accepted, we can enjoy relationships without the pressure and disappointment of trying to make a person meet needs only God can.

> IF OUR BASIC NEEDS ARE MET IN HIM, WE CAN APPROACH HUMAN RELATIONSHIP FOR PLEASURE RATHER THAN NEED.

> *Yet I am never alone, for the Father is always with me. And everything I've taught you is so that the peace which is in me will be in you and will give you great confidence as you rest in me. For in this unbelieving world you will experience trouble and sorrows, but you must be courageous, for I have conquered the world!*
> John 16:32b-33

Perhaps we suspect this change in the purpose of relationships means we remain aloof to people. Jesus, however, was vulnerable to people to the point of death. His love went deep, and He allowed people to hurt Him. He was in no way aloof or unfeeling. This potential for rejection and pain did not dissuade Him from serving us and dying for us while we were

His hateful enemies (Romans 5:8). We don't need to withdraw or pretend, hiding behind a façade we think will keep us safe. Instead, we can be real. Jesus was never afraid of being awkward or rejected. He was always exactly who He was. This, I suggest, is only possible for us when we find our identity in Him, just as He found His identity in His Father (John 14:20). Finding our identity in Him means allowing Him to define us as we live in relationship with Him and as He empowers us to live.

Where's the Love?

> *So I give you now a new commandment: Love each other just as much as I have loved you. For when you demonstrate the same love I have for you by loving one another, everyone will know that you're my true followers.*
>
> *John 13:34*

How do we love one another when we are in a world full of crazy people who seem hell-bent on hurting us? When the love of Jesus fills us and spills over to others, loving people becomes a natural outflow rather than a strenuous effort. The fruit of the Spirit is His fruit, not ours. As He lives within us, this love overflows to all around us to those who need it. Importantly, this love isn't something of our own making or something "deserved" by them.

> *Then one of them, a religious scholar, posed this question to test him: "Teacher, which commandment in the law is the greatest?" Jesus answered him, "'Love the Lord your God with every passion of your heart, with all the energy of your being, and with every thought that is within you.' This is the great and supreme commandment. And the second is like it in importance: 'You must love your friend in the same way you love yourself.' Contained within these commandments to love you will find all the meaning of the Law and the Prophets."*
>
> *Matthew 22:35–40*

Demonstrated love doesn't look the same for everyone. It is not necessarily mushy-gushy. Sometimes we confuse genuine love with people-pleasing. If we ask God to reveal just how to love the person in front of us in their specific circumstance, He will. It may not make sense to us, but He knows hearts and speaks the language of love directly to their hearts. We just get to meet Him there. This takes the pressure off us to know what love looks like in every situation.

One of my mentors in college talked about three different categories of friendship. What he said has helped me to understand my role in each of the categories. The first is a giving relationship, when you are investing in another person. It is a one-way street, and you are doing the work. The second is the reverse of this, a receiving relationship in which the other person invests in you while you are not reciprocating. The third (and much smaller group typically) is a sharing relationship in which you and the other person mutually invest in each other. Many people become overwhelmed by having too many people in the first category and resent the recipients' failure to reciprocate. However, if these relationships are to remain in such imbalance, you can assign them to the ministry category and avoid disappointment when those you help don't help you in return. It is important to remember, however, that you cannot invest in everyone nor does God call you to do so.

We are called to maintain our connection with the Church (the family of God). With the call of God comes His provision to maintain this connection, even when the friendship base isn't there all the time. He fills us with love and acceptance, empowering us to approach whomever He has incorporated into our lives with His love. They may not be lovable or meet our criteria of "deserving" of it, but we know we will have enough because God has called us to them. We remain connected with the Church, not because it is perfect or because the Church serves us, but because God asks us to.

Relationship with people depends completely on relationship with God, and when we get the order right, we can move forward in healthy human relationship. When we try to get a person to fill the needs that only God can as we live abiding in Him, we get frustrated and disappointed because that person cannot fulfill us in this way. As we live in connection with God, allowing Him to define us, provide for all our needs, and empower us to do the impossible, God enables us to relate with people in the way He intended.

Going Deeper:

1. What relationships have become idols in your life?

2. What relationships has God called you to that you are resisting because you are afraid? Who is God calling you away from because your fear of losing the relationship has become an idol?

3. What relationships in the past have you tried to use to identify yourself, requiring the other person to give you perfect love and acceptance? Were you offended when they failed to meet your expectations?

4. Do you have friendships in all three categories (giving, receiving, and sharing)? Do you have too many in one of those? Too few?

5. Ask God to reveal how He will love those in your life by enabling you to love in a way that is far beyond anything you could ever do yourself.

Breaking Free

Hannah Morrell

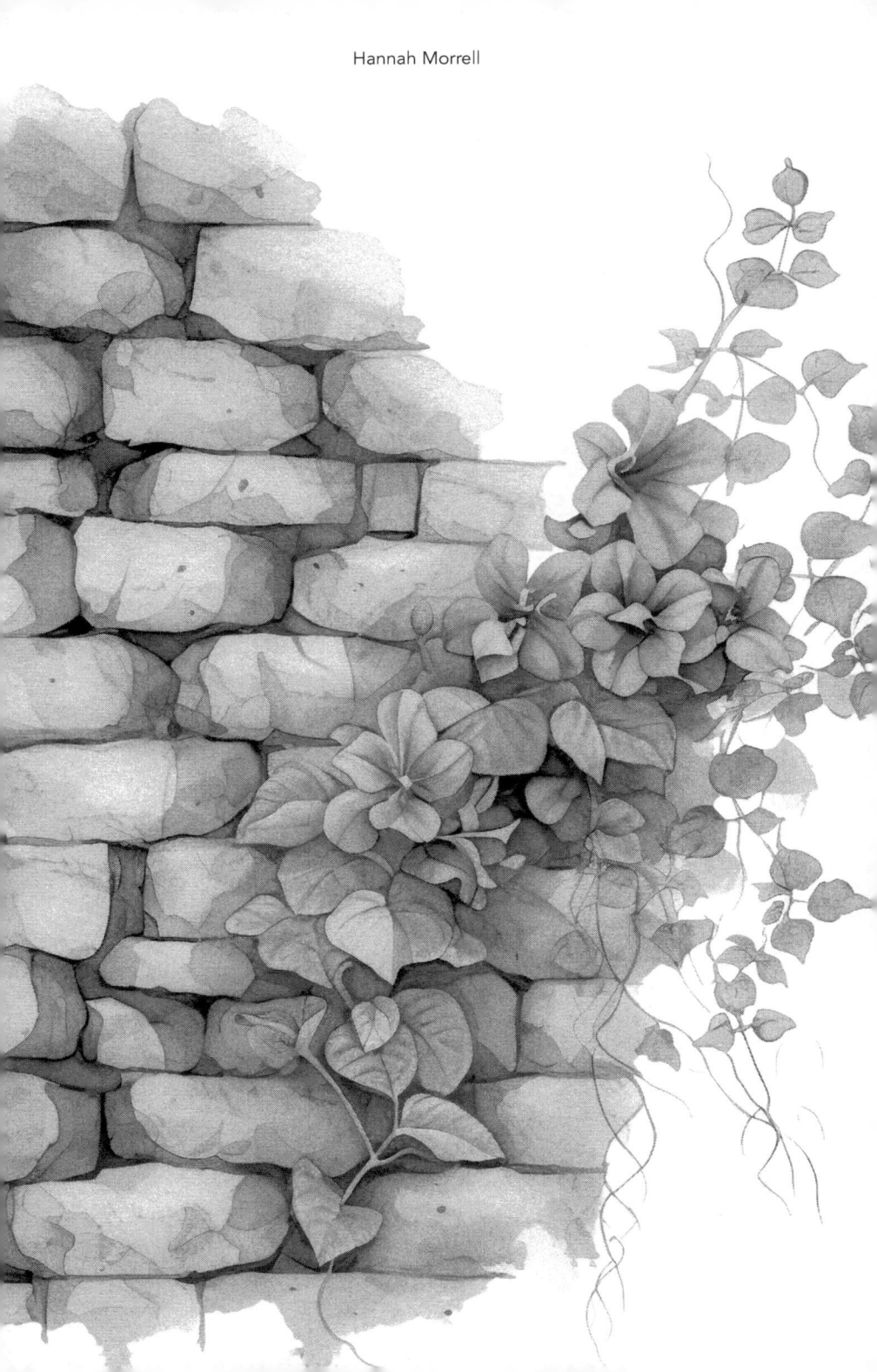

What Do I Do With Myself?

Jesus Christ is able to untangle all the snarls in your soul, to banish all your complexes, and to transform even your fixed habit patterns, no matter how deeply they are etched in your subconscious.
—Corrie Ten Boom[23]

How do I live with myself and all the repercussions of the past, whether because of my own failures or because of hurts brought by others? I think we start by acknowledging that life is not intended to be a straight line of perfect choices. We often portray God as expecting a straight-line life from us. Really, I believe He wants relationship with us, not perfection brought about by our own fleshly determination. This is why the Bible often contrasts the sinner with the religious, claiming it's better to be the sinner because sinners recognize their need for a Savior while the religious focus on being good enough in their own strength and power.

My emotions sometimes tell me I'm a worthless, hopeless failure—but that isn't God's truth. Emotions aren't bad, and I think we have made them out to be. Feelings are great warning

---

[23] ten Boom, Corrie. *Amazing Love: True Stories of the Power of Forgiveness*. CLC Publications, 2018.

lights of what is going on, but they shouldn't be in charge. If we allow our emotions to dictate truth, we are in a mess. If I have a dream that my husband cheated on me and wake up angry at him, this is an emotion that is not based on truth. I get to lead that emotion gently to a place where I acknowledge my husband has been faithful, that he loves me, and that he did not cheat on me as I dreamed. My anger will eventually dissipate and allow me to see clearly without squashing or denying my feelings. Truth must lead emotion tenderly.

When we talked about flesh patterns in Chapter 3, we discussed acknowledging not only the lies that are imbedded in us but also God's truth replacing the lies.

- I am a beloved delight—not a disappointment. (Romans 8:38)
- I am rejoiced over with singing—not a bother. (Zephaniah 3:17)
- I am seated in the heavenlies—not a cowering disaster. (Ephesians 2:6)
- I am given worth—not trying to earn it constantly. (Romans 5:1–2)
- I am one whose value is in Who I belong to—not how productive or "good" I am. (Ephesians 2:8–9)
- I am led by a Good Shepherd—not grasping for control or power in an attempt to be my own god. (Psalm 23)

I am in relationship with my Heavenly Father, my Jesus, my Holy Spirit—not trying to figure out my life by trying to make Him happy with my religious zeal. (Isaiah 41:10)

Breaking Free

The world's definition of success might be a good job, plenty of money, an attractive spouse or children, or power in government. God's definition of success is knowing Him!

> GOD'S DEFINITION OF SUCCESS IS KNOWING HIM!

> *Eternal life means to know and experience you as the only true God, and to know and experience Jesus Christ, as the Son whom you have sent.*
>
> *John 17:3*

Getting Rid of the Lies

> *Yet all of the accomplishments that I once took credit for, I've now forsaken them and I regard it all as nothing compared to the delight of experiencing Jesus Christ as my Lord! To truly know him meant letting go of everything from my past and throwing all my boasting on the garbage heap. It's all like a pile of manure to me now, so that I may be enriched in the reality of knowing Jesus Christ and embrace him as Lord in all of his greatness.*
>
> *Philippians 3:7–8*

God always puts us in the best place to know Him, for that's His goal for us and His definition of success and completion. It may not feel like the best place to know Him, but we don't have His perspective. He defines us, so knowing Him is really knowing ourselves as well. As we grow to know Him, we can rest in the love He has for us rather than fighting all the lies that have defined us for so long.

I must get rid of the lies that define me from my past and pursue the truth of who God says I am. This is a bit of work and sometimes feels like a never-ending process. But no lie or pain is too much for God's healing power. He is the One who can free us from every entanglement, every trauma, and every lie spoken over us.

How do we rid ourselves of the lies? We first acknowledge and identify them as God brings them to the forefront. Then, we inject truth into them—the truth that God gives to identify who we are as a new person with His Life within. It may take some time to stop reacting to the lies, but slowly we see them for what they are—untruths that control our behavior and our beliefs about ourselves.

In dismissing the lies, we can come back to abiding and connection with Jesus more quickly and stay there longer. We don't get as distracted by the untruths and horrible messages that plague us because we don't give them time or try to prove them wrong. Instead, we move into the truth of our identity in Christ, completely connected and abiding in Him.

Finding Your Calling

And if anyone longs to be wise, ask God for wisdom and he will give it! He won't see your lack of wisdom as an opportunity to scold you over your failures but he will overwhelm your failures with his generous grace.
James 1:5

How do you find your calling and purpose in life? The number of times I have heard this question tells me it is an important concern in any age group. I've often said I wished colleges had a class on sustainable living in a career. A girl who had just graduated came to me and asked, "Now what?" After much educational effort, starting a career, and not feeling fulfilled or able to keep going at that pace, she was a little confused. Is it a rinse and repeat? We pull all-nighters, get sick on breaks after finals because we've been too busy during the term to get sick, and keep pouring time and money into something. And then? We just start a new life with no idea what to do to move from survival mode into something sustainable.

This can happen in other seasons of life after we have figured out how to make it through an intense experience but don't know how to live life in a way that makes sense following that. So, how do we move into living life rather than just existing?

Ask God first.

So often we are looking everywhere for guidance instead of to the One who calls us to Himself first. As you ask God about this calling, look at how He is leading in the natural. Do you like people? Do you like fixing things? Do you like teaching others?

My friend Mike Wells used to travel at least 300 days a year to all sorts of exotic places, teaching people and counseling them in relationship with Jesus. I asked him one day how he chose where he went the next year, thinking that it would be a very involved formula for determining God's will for his schedule. Mike told me he asked God about the next year, thought about what would be the most fun, and then scheduled travel to that place!

I couldn't believe you could do that! I thought that God really had a miserable plan for my life and didn't understand that

He often leads in the natural—the things you love, the things you are passionate about. Pay attention to those rather than expecting things to always be difficult. Yes, He calls us through valleys of pain sometimes, but I don't believe we should choose misery because we believe doing so is more spiritual.

Another area to evaluate is letting God cut things off in His time. Just because you've been doing something for years, or something has worked ok until now, doesn't mean it is still what He is calling you to do. Check in with your heart to see if you are doing something because you think people expect it of you, because you will get acceptance or approval because of it, or because you are comfortable there.

I know this may seem like a stupid question, but have you realized you may change your mind throughout your life? Just because you have started in one direction doesn't mean you have to continue in the same direction. Some personalities definitely struggle more with this sense of loyalty to or permanence in their decisions. There are decisions I would recommend committing to—God, marriage, kids, friends. But sometimes God will call you to a different path, maybe a different job, a different health journey, a different place. If we are falsely loyal to something, we can refuse to go when it's time. Be open to having God change your mind.

So many believers are stressed about being in God's will and in finding it out. I don't believe that God's will is found in a particular person, place or thing, but rather in a heart attitude towards Him. Yes, He is involved in the details of our lives, but the order must be right. The heart comes before behavior every time in God's economy. If we are turning our hearts towards Him in softness and with a desire to be in relationship with Him as primary, the rest follows and isn't nearly as stressful. We also don't have to worry about messing up, because we are trusting and entrusting through every decision that God is taking us through and sorting things out.

Standing Faithful

I know what it means to lack, and I know what it means to experience overwhelming abundance. For I'm trained in the secret of overcoming all things, whether in fullness or in hunger. And I find that the strength of Christ's explosive power infuses me to conquer every difficulty.
Philippians 4:12–13

Once you determine your calling in the now, sometimes it is hard to stay faithful. Standing firm on those days when you want to run away and never come back can be difficult. I have those days, and I realize He provides my faithfulness just as He does my calling! He makes our feet stay steadfast.

It also helps to remember that our approval comes from Jesus first. There is a story of a famous pianist who was playing his heart out on his piano through an amazing repertoire for a massive audience one evening. At the end of his performance, the audience gave him a standing ovation. But the pianist didn't look at the crowd. He was intently searching the top balcony for a sight of one elderly man—the piano teacher of his youth—who had come to hear him play that night. The pianist was playing for an audience of one. Your audience of One is Him. Play for Him and be empowered by Him.

Success or failure isn't up to us because God empowers us to do everything and gets all the credit. If we choose to wear our failure, that will take us down. We must leave success or failure in His hands and trust Him for the outcome.

I remember one day asking God for an encouraging email to lift my spirits, as I was quite discouraged. I received one. It was a sweet note detailing the impact ministry had in a person's life, and I was loving it. God whispered to me in the silence after reading the email: *How long will this one last?* I realized at that moment that, realistically, I would need another in about 15 minutes—the fulfillment didn't last. Don't get me wrong; I do like encouragement, but God must be the source of what I do, as well as the One whom I trust when good or bad seems to happen. He is the Faithful One who is working in people, and I just get to show up where He has already worked, speak His words, and meet Him there. How great is that?

I believe it is also important to learn contentedness. Learning to be content is more possible when we choose not to determine value by what others think of us. I think this comes with practicing gratitude and running away from comparison. When we look around and thank God for what we have and where we are, acknowledging every bit is from Him, we find contentment. And when we run from comparing ourselves with others for any reason, we can find rest and genuine love for these people. We cannot compare or judge (to compare ourselves to others, we first have to judge them) and love at the same time.

Breaking Free

I greatly admire many of the words of Corrie ten Boom, a woman who survived prison camp in World War II, and traveled the world preaching forgiveness and Jesus's love. This is what she said about starting an international ministry in her 50s after losing her whole family and watching her country shredded by war.

> My job was simply to follow His leading one step at a time, holding every decision up to Him in prayer.
> —Corrie ten Boom[24]

So simple! I overcomplicate all of it and exhaust myself in the process.

When you want to quit and run away, come to Him for refreshment. Recognize all of us deal with this at some point, and it's not because we are failures. I received an email one day from a friend in ministry who was ready to quit. He was discouraged, disillusioned, and ready to be done with everything involving the ministry. When others who are supposed to have your back reject or hurt you, it's easy to go to that same place of discouragement. By the next day, I received a follow-up email with the simple message that he was doing ok because Jesus had refreshed him. He was back in a place of recognizing that the place of weakness wasn't to be run from, but pushed into so that Christ could be his strength in it.

It's also ok to take a break from healing, from emotional work, from problems, and from physical work. We all need to take breaks to just be and to rest and be restored before we move further. I think sometimes we imagine we must always be

---
[24] ten Boom, Corrie, et al. *The Hiding Place*. United States, Baker Publishing Group, 2006. 99.

doing something, but Jesus took time away with His Father so often throughout His walking the earth. He was quick to take a break, get quiet, and allow His Father (and ours) to restore His soul. We have a Shepherd who encourages us to come to Him with weariness and being heavy-laden so that He can provide rest (Matthew 11:28–30).

Grieving broken dreams must also be allowed. Grieving is important but is something many cultures (including North American) do not do a good job of acknowledging. I think sometimes we just need to be sad and allow all the emotions associated with the loss to come pouring out. We do this with Jesus, not in spite of Him or while hiding it from Him. Jesus grieves with us, as He understands emotion and has compassion.

I like to take ten minutes each day to sit in grief when I'm in the heavy seasons of it. I let myself sit in emotion and feel sad or angry or whatever I need to feel for that time. Then, I reset by saying something like, "You are welcome here, Father, Son and Spirit, and I'm glad You are giving me what I need to get through today," or sometimes I look at a picture (like a flower blooming, or a beautiful beach where I feel peace) that helps me come back to life and reenter. I like to look at this time of grieving as piling all my stuff up and putting it on Jesus' lap for Him to deal with.

Remember, the goal in life isn't to do everything you wanted, or to never miss out on anything. God's goal for this life is that you know Him. It's very relational, and it is truly amazing that God wants us above all else. He doesn't treat us like someone to be tolerated, but genuinely enjoys relationship with us. Abiding life is good for us, and we have everything we need when we recognize our connection to God as a branch on the Vine (John 15).

> HE DOESN'T TREAT US LIKE SOMEONE TO BE TOLERATED BUT GENUINELY ENJOYS RELATIONSHIP WITH US.

You Can't Always Get What You Want

As for us, we have all of these great witnesses who encircle us like clouds. So we must let go of every wound that has pierced us and the sin we so easily fall into. Then we will be able to run life's marathon race with passion and determination, for the path has been already marked out before us. We look away from the natural realm and we focus our attention and expectation onto Jesus who birthed faith within us and who leads us forward into faith's perfection. His example is this: Because his heart was focused on the joy of knowing that you would be his, he endured the agony of the cross and conquered its humiliation, and now sits exalted at the right hand of the throne of God!

Hebrews 12:1–2

What do you do when you don't get what you want? Remember, you are not alone. Many others have not received the thing they prayed for, wanted, ached for. In Hebrews 11, the writer lists many who died without receiving the gift they desired most: their promised Messiah, Jesus. The writer calls these people blessed! Scripture shows us that God values faith.

Letting go of the natural realm as the thing that will make us happy is important as well. We often feel that just getting the next thing will bring satisfaction. We can try a different spouse, a different job, more money, more power, or a totally different life in a totally different place. None of them satisfies. This is why we can sometimes meet people who have exactly what we think we want and find that they are unfulfilled or dissatisfied. They have reached this so-called pinnacle and are still striving for something else. I believe that only in God can we find satisfaction, as that's what He created us for.

If you don't find what you wanted in the natural realm, grieve it, and leave it with Jesus. Then push into the spiritual realm and feel your heart explode! I know that when I was trying to find all the things that were supposed to make me happy, I never knew joy or contentment like I do when I am pursuing and spending time with the Lover of my soul. God knows how to meet our spirits and encourage them to crave something more than what we can find in this world. This isn't a tease or a prank, but a calling to come up above and recognize who we are already and Who loves us so much already.

God will fulfill His promises to us, but not necessarily in the way you expect. We may have to let go of getting what we want in the way or time we want it. I think of Joseph after being sold by his brothers into slavery, serving in a house faithfully, and turning down the advances of his master's wife. He then goes to prison for something he didn't do, forgotten by those whom he had helped (Genesis 39). Yes, God's goal was to bring him to power at Pharaoh's side, but I am not sure the path to that position was quite the one Joseph expected after his dreams of ruling over his brothers (Genesis 37)! God kept His promise, but definitely not in the way or timeline expected. He is always faithful, though, and will continue to bring us through.

Breaking Free

Relationship with God teaches us a different way of doing life, one in which God's Truth for us controls us, and lies cannot. We can stand faithful and move deeper in relationship with Him as He enables us to do so. Even when we don't get what we want, we can look past the natural to the reality of the spiritual. This way of living frees us to move beyond the pain of the past, the discomfort of the present, and the fear of the future into a simple walk of trust and sweet connection with the Lover of our souls. He invites us into relationship constantly, and life is much better when we accept the invitation.

Going Deeper:

1. Spend some time meditating on how you let go of the lies of the identity of the past and move more and more into the identity Jesus gives you—His beloved one.

2. What is your calling right now as defined by God? This isn't necessarily a career, but a place in which you feel led to serve, finding some fulfillment and experiencing growth.

3. How is God bringing contentment, no matter where you are?

4. Spend some time telling God about the things that you want but have not received. Leave them with Him.

5. How does moving into God's definition of success (knowing Him) change your outlook on the future?

Hannah Morrell

What Do We Do With Suffering?

> *It is as though suffering is a strange sort of gift from God, a gift that we reluctantly receive and constantly want to give back. But it has extraordinary power to change us. It changes our outlook, our faith, our walk with God.*
>
> —Vaneetha Risner[25]

I have had many times of crisis in my life when I have felt as if my heart would crack apart, either from my own suffering or from witnessing suffering in the lives of others. Amid so much pain, I have questioned God's love and His desire for relationship. There are many others with whom I have talked who feel, or have felt, similarly and ask me how a loving God could allow suffering.

I am not planning to answer all these questions in this chapter, but I want to share what I believe about suffering. It is an important topic and one that comes up often in many areas of our lives. I will also reference the perspectives of others on the topic, as there are some who have suffered more than I could dream possible and have incredible wisdom on the

---

[25] Risner, Vaneetha. "Where is God in the Dark?" *Crossmap Blogs*. June 26, 2014. https://blogs.crossmap.com/stories/where-is-god-in-the-dark-vaneetha-risner-6IY0hoWlwPkYKKawEoD_x

subject. We must have a theology of suffering in order to accept relationship with God, understanding that it isn't punishment or misery on purpose for us.

Suffering is Normal

And everything I've taught you is so that the peace which is in me will be in you and will give you great confidence as you rest in me. For in this unbelieving world you will experience trouble and sorrows, but you must be courageous, for I have conquered the world!
John 16:33

First, we must recognize that suffering is a normal part of life, not necessarily something caused by our behavior or lack of faith. Jesus told us to expect it.

If Paul, Peter, and other heroes of the faith suffered (to the point of death, no less), how do we expect we will not? While they were sinful men, just like any other, their suffering wasn't punishment from God, as they suffered *for* God. In the same way, we can't say that all suffering is punishment from God; this isn't the way God works. He can always bring good out of the suffering, though, and it is not the end of the story (Romans 8:28).

On the cross, Jesus bore and dealt with the punishment for sin, so now, God purposes suffering to draw us deeper into relationship with Him. He suffered more than any other human and considered pursuing us in relationship worth all the pain (Philippians 2:6–8).

Breaking Free
Asking the Wrong Question

> *Beloved friends, what should be our proper response to God's marvelous mercies? To surrender yourselves to God to be his sacred, living sacrifices. And live in holiness, experiencing all that delights his heart. For this becomes your genuine expression of worship.*
> Romans 12:1–2

Second, I believe that we often ask the wrong question. Answering the "why" of suffering isn't really the answer we want. So often we think that if we could figure out why we are suffering, blame it on a behavior or a choice or just an angry god, we would feel better. But it doesn't work that way. Even if I can explain why someone mistreated me, I don't feel better about the mistreatment. Often, I don't have the perspective that God has either, so when I consider a particular experience to be awful, I must also recognize that I have not yet seen the end of the story.

You are in good company in asking for suffering's explanation as David, Job, Moses, and many other people in the Bible asked God why they felt abandoned or continued to suffer. But I find that God rarely gives them (or us) a direct answer on the why. Here's what Ann Voskamp has to say about it:

> *All your suffering isn't some unique anomaly, suffering is the universal experience of all humanity. Suffering doesn't mean you're cursed, suffering means you're human.*
>
> *The question isn't "Why is there brokenness and suffering in my life?"—but "Why wouldn't there be suffering because such is life in a broken world?" Buy the lie that your life is supposed to be heaven on earth, and suffering can be a torturous hell. But accept and expect that life is a battle, then suffering isn't a problem but part of earth's topography to cross on our way to heaven. There is no point trying*

to *question* suffering, the point is how are you going to *answer* suffering. The question never is if you understand the *why* of your suffering — and the answer always is *how* are you going to stand up and walk *through* your suffering. You don't have to know the *reason* for your suffering—you only have to know your *response* through the suffering. And this has to be my response to suffering: Surrender.

Surrender and bravely open your arms cruciform and *welcome* whatever comes.

Our openhanded *welcome* to *whatever* comes invites healing wellness to come.

Surrender to His Story and welcome the Author Himself and whatever Word He brings. Wellness comes as we welcome the Word and whatever line He writes into our story.

God's promises never claim we won't be afflicted; He promises we will never be evicted from God's presence. This is always enough. I wrap this comfort around myself when my aching heart forgets again and again.

—Ann Voskamp[26]

Instead of asking why, Ann suggests we pursue the how of walking forward. Surrender is never our immediate response, but it allows us to move back to relationship with God rather than trying to orchestrate our own freedom from suffering.

> WHEN WE SURRENDER AND WALK IN DEPENDENCE, WE ALLOW JESUS TO BE ALL WE NEED...

We recognize He is carrying us through and will never stop doing that. I think that abiding life allows us access to all the resources we need to make it through difficult times, and this becomes the how. When we surrender and walk in dependence, we allow Jesus to be all we need through us, whether we are suffering or not.

---

26 Voskamp, Ann. *WayMaker: Finding the Way to the Life You've Always Dreamed Of.* United States, Thomas Nelson, 2022. 10.

Breaking Free
Never Alone

> *He has done this intentionally so that every member would look after the others with mutual concern, and so that there will be no division in the body. In that way, whatever happens to one member happens to all. If one suffers, everyone suffers. If one is honored, everyone rejoices.*
>
> 1 Corinthians 12:25–26

Third, we are not alone in suffering. I often wish I could just gather those with whom I talk and ask them to talk to each other to help everyone understand they are not alone in the struggle. We look at suffering as being something that we alone deal with, that no one else can understand. This is completely untrue, and often, when we can listen to the stories of others, we comprehend that many have suffered on a level beyond our deepest imaginings. This isn't a misery-loves-company mentality, but an understanding that suffering is normal for the children of God and that there is purpose in it.

Part of being in relationship with the Church is the shared suffering, which allows us to experience healthy human relationships as God intended. I love the intentionality God has in creating the Church so that members will take care of each other, suffer together, and rejoice together. This is how the Church is supposed to function and support each other. When we are living in relationship with God and getting our needs met through Him, we can operate in the Church out of that empowerment of God. This means that we are never alone, as we have God with us all the time, and the Church surrounds us with support as well. I realize the Church does not always function the way it's supposed to, but when we are filled up with relationship with Jesus, anything people give us is icing on the cake.

The Promise of Comfort

All praises belong to the God and Father of our Lord Jesus Christ. For he is the Father of tender mercy and the God of endless comfort. He always comes alongside us to comfort us in every suffering so that we can come alongside those who are in any painful trial. We can bring them this same comfort that God has poured out upon us.
2 Corinthians 1:3–4

God promises many things in suffering. He says He will be with us in it and comfort us through it. He is not absent emotionally, as we so often assume.

My friend and mentor died suddenly in 2011, three months after my son was born. I was crushed, not knowing what to do with my grief and trying to support my newborn while figuring out my life without a man who had loved me so well and was supposed to be a bonus grandfather to my child. We received the news of Mike's death while we were standing in baggage claim at the airport, coming back from a trip to Hawaii that he had gifted us. I remember driving back home in a fog, trying to figure out if this could be real.

We drove straight to the home of Mike's son, wanting to be with his family and close as we grieved together. I sat on the floor in a room, trying to nurse my 3-month-old son and feeling as if my body couldn't continue to function as it was supposed to. My little son reached his tiny hand up and put it on my cheek, resting it there momentarily. He didn't really have control of his limbs much at that point, but I know it was God reaching through this little one to comfort me. I wept as I nursed my son.

God has never been absent emotionally, even in the darkest, hardest moments for me. He has always comforted, whether through others, or just in the quiet sweetness of His love for me. He does this for each of us, knowing that we need this emotional connection in relationship with Him.

The Promise of Fruit Produced in Suffering

> But that's not all! Even in times of trouble we have a joyful confidence, knowing that our pressures will develop in us patient endurance. And patient endurance will refine our character, and proven character leads us back to hope. And this hope is not a disappointing fantasy, because we can now experience the endless love of God cascading into our hearts through the Holy Spirit who lives in us!
>
> Romans 5:3–5

Another promise of God in suffering is that it is productive. Yes, I said productive. I know we don't like it, but suffering is where we come close to Jesus and often where we know Him best. I know the hardest times in my life have been times when I know God like I've never known Him before. I sometimes compare it to human relationships—the people with whom I am the closest and enjoy the deepest relationships are generally those with whom I have been through some trials and struggles, and our relationship has come out the other side.

Joni Eareckson Tada, a quadriplegic who has experienced multiple cancer battles, has a lot of interesting thoughts on suffering, and I would say she has definitely earned the right to speak on it.

> Somehow, in the midst of your suffering, the Son of God beckons you into the inner sanctum of His own suffering—a place of mystery and privilege you will never forget. I have suffered, yes. But I wouldn't trade places with anybody in the world to be this close to Jesus.
> —Joni Eareckson Tada[27]

We share suffering with other people, but also with Jesus Himself. This means we also share in the revelation of His glory (1 Peter 4:12–13). Have you ever considered that suffering allows us to share in glory? There is something about it that buys our place in celebrating the wins of God's glory as we see them. It's sort of like being on a winning football team and having earned the championship trophy because we have fought hard with blood, sweat, and tears. We don't just experience the hard stuff—we get the good stuff too!

Surviving Suffering

> I am convinced that any suffering we endure is less than nothing compared to the magnitude of glory that is about to be unveiled within us. The entire universe is standing on tiptoe, yearning to see the unveiling of God's glorious sons and daughters!
> Romans 8:18–19

How do we survive suffering? I think we first need to allow people to suffer, rather than blaming them or trying to fix it for them. We need to allow it in ourselves as well. We often don't know how to lament. It is ok to be sad and to let God comfort

---

27 Tada, Joni Eareckson. *Beside Bethesda: 31 Days toward Deeper Healing.* Colorado Springs, NavPress, 2014. 81.

you. When we determine it's not ok to be sad or angry, we neglect and try to shut down some very important emotions.

Too many times, I have witnessed someone give a trite answer to people who are in pain, trying to dismiss it and make them "feel better." But this doesn't allow for grief or lament at all. I love in the Psalms how David goes through a whole variety of emotions—sadness, anguish, anger, joy, elation. He doesn't limit himself to expressing only the "positive" emotions, as they seem to be called. David was called a man after God's own heart (1 Samuel 13:14), and I believe this is partly because of his emotions. We need to make space for lament in our own lives and in the lives of those around us.

Vaneetha Risner is a woman who has written several books about suffering and has walked an incredibly hard road with a child's death, divorce, physical disability, and post-polio syndrome. She says:

> The Bible is shockingly honest. And because of that, I can be honest as well. I can both complain and cry, knowing that God can handle anything I say. The Lord wants me to talk to him, pour out my heart and my thoughts unedited because He knows them already.
> —Vaneetha Risner[28]

When you are dealing with suffering, it is sometimes helpful to remember your altars. By altars, I mean those places you have seen God work in the past and for which you have erected some sort of mental altar to remind you. In the Old Testament, God often had His people set up altars to remember what He had done or where He had delivered them because He knew

---

[28] Risner, Vaneetha. "The Necessity of Lament." *Dancing in the Rain*. Vaneetha Risner: August 20, 2015. https://www.danceintherain.com/blog-archive/2015/08/20/the-necessity-of-lament

humans were quick to forget. We need altars also, but they can come in many forms: a journal entry, a note on your phone, or a picture or tangible object.

Often in the middle of suffering, the last thing we want to do is praise and worship. We want the conclusion, the happy ending, the resolution. Then, and only then, we might feel inclined to praise God. There is something about praising in the middle of a situation of suffering, though, that changes us. We aren't worshipping BECAUSE we are suffering, but we are turning our eyes and hearts towards the One Who will bring us through and Who deserves to be worshipped. We don't have to live in fear or discouragement because we know He will be enough for us all the way through.

In Acts 16, Paul and Silas were praying and singing hymns in prison. They didn't sing and pray once they had experienced freedom from jail, but while they were still inside. We don't worship and praise because we feel like it but because we look up and over the problem to the One who holds us and carries us through.

I recorded a podcast called "Undercurrents of Hope" and called my first season "In the Middle." I have a great desire to share the stories of people who are still in the thick of their story without finding resolution but see God's goodness and love in the middle. This is such an encouragement to those of us who may not have completed a journey yet and are still without a happy ending. We can still find hope in the middle.

Breaking Free

One thing I tell people who are suffering is that it's ok to let the moments get small. By that I mean right now, you may not be able to think about tomorrow, next week, or next month. You can take things one moment at a time, even if the moments feel huge when you are in the middle of suffering. Overwhelm is real when you move ahead of what you are ready for right now.

Kara Tippetts was a mother of four who fought through cancer for several years and wrote about her story as she went. She allowed us an incredibly vulnerable view into her pain, her hope, and her struggle. Here's what she said about staying in the present small moments.

> *Hard is grace too. Don't imagine yourself in the future, because that is you without the grace provided for that moment. There is peace for this day, find it.*
>
> —*Kara Tippetts*[29]

Remember that no matter the suffering, peace is a Person, and no one can take Him away from you. Push into peace—you have access to Him anytime, any day, anywhere. You don't have to wait until the suffering ends to have hope and peace, for you have Jesus all the time. He brings peace and hope into any situation and allows you to see past it. Here's Kara again:

> *My hope is not in the absence of suffering and comfort returned. My hope is in the presence of the One who promises never to leave or forsake, the One who declares nothing will be able to separate us from the love of God. Nothing.*
>
> —*Kara Tippetts*[30]

---

[29] Tippetts, Kara. "A Big Pill." *Mundane Faithfulness.* December 13, 2012. https://www.mundanefaithfulness.com/home/2012/12/13/a-big-pill
[30] Tippetts, Kara. *The Hardest Peace: Expecting Grace in the Midst of Life's Hard.* United States, David C Cook, 2014. 78.

Mike Wells used to talk about how, when he was traveling all over the world, he noticed people in third-world countries found fulfillment in spiritual things because that was the only place they had any freedom. Many of these people are born into their careers, parents arrange their marriages, and they don't have the finances or liberty to travel or move. So, instead of pursuing many of the things we in western countries use to find fulfillment, they pursue spirituality.

We really are the same, but sometimes fail to recognize it. We have no limits spiritually, regardless of our circumstance. We can always access the throne of grace with boldness (Hebrews 4:16), and we will always find Jesus with us.

Remember in suffering that this life is not designed for comfort (although sometimes I wish it were!) but rather to know God. Eternal life is knowing God (John 17:3), and we often grow in relationship in the middle of hard things. I like to think of this life as a bootcamp, a preparation for the main event. We can have a relationship with God now, and we don't need to be comfortable to move into this more deeply. God knows how to prepare us for what's next, and He knows that when we pursue Him, as His bride, we have all we need for this life.

Don't beat up on yourself or others when you find yourself in suffering. This is unhelpful and distracting. We often become obsessed with the struggle—what did I do wrong to cause this, or what lesson do I need to learn to get rid of it? This puts us in a place of trying to understand something that only God has the perspective to understand, and we can drive ourselves crazy. Don't compare to someone else's suffering either. It doesn't make you feel any better, and it doesn't help them. Whatever journey God has put in front of you, He will walk with you the whole way and empower you to make it through. He has not empowered you for someone else's journey.

In a private meeting, Brian Simmons, lead translator of the Passion Translation and pastor, shared that nothing in the Christian life starts with doing, but rather yielding. We tend to get the order wrong and forget that the source of good works or bringing life to others is Jesus. We don't do good to get to Him; He empowers any good in us. Jesus entrusted His Spirit to God, for He is the only safe place. Surrender allows freedom, as we are no longer trying to grasp onto anything we think will help. As you commit and entrust your life to Him, He takes care of you and leads you through. He is the only safe place.

Surrendering to God is not giving up. Sometimes people end up in a suicidal place when they think it's best to just give up. We can see that we are unable, or think

> SURRENDERING TO HIM IS ENTRUSTING TO HIM THAT WHICH IS PRECIOUS TO YOU, ACKNOWLEDGING HE IS BETTER AT TAKING CARE OF THEM THAN YOU ARE.

we need to acquire knowledge to get through the suffering. But we must move further and see that God is still active and working and moving things to surround us in love all the way through. Surrendering to Him is entrusting to Him that which is precious to you, acknowledging He is better at taking care of it than you are.

Remember God's promises and keep coming to Him for their fulfillment. He knows what He has promised, and I think

He loves it when we come to Him with His own words. He has promised to see us through to completion, and to take care of the beginning and middle as well. He is faithful and will bring it to pass (Philippians 1:6).

There is something incredibly sweet in the times of dependence on God, although sometimes it feels like death. When we have nothing else and, in surrender, throw ourselves on His everlasting arms, we realize He has been with us all along and loves to take care of us. He meets us with love, with delight, with welcome. He loves it when you turn to Him and wait for what He will do. Suffering is not something we look forward to, but we can enjoy the tenderness of relationship with God Triune in the middle. The Father bends close. The Son sheds tears of compassion, and the Spirit lifts us up in encouragement and hope. It may be hard to see in suffering, but God loves you so much. Relationship develops in times of hardship, and we can move deeper in abiding in Christ through the suffering if we allow it to lead us there.

Breaking Free
Going Deeper:

1. What suffering in the present or past do you need to lament before God? Spend some time pouring out your heart to Him about the sadness and leave it with Him.
2. What encourages you to praise God in the storm when you haven't found the resolution yet?
3. What blame do you need to let go of for suffering in your life, whether directed at yourself or others?
4. What promises from God do you need to hold on to as you surrender this suffering to Him?
5. How do you come to a place of worship and praise when you don't feel like it?
6. Meditate on these other verses about suffering and allow God to speak to you about the place in which you find yourself right now.

My fellow believers, when it seems as though you are facing nothing but difficulties, see it as an invaluable opportunity to experience the greatest joy that you can! For you know that when your faith is tested it stirs up in you the power of endurance. And then as your endurance grows even stronger, it will release perfection into every part of your being until there is nothing missing and nothing lacking.
James 1:2–4

Beloved friends, if life gets extremely difficult, with many tests, don't be bewildered as though something strange were overwhelming you. Instead, continue to rejoice, for you, in a measure, have shared in the sufferings of the Anointed One so that you can share in the revelation of his glory and celebrate with even greater gladness!
1 Peter 4:12–13

Hannah Morrell

How Do We Live With Hope in Our Present?

> When your identity is in Christ, your identity is the same yesterday, today and tomorrow. Criticism can't change it. Failing can't shake it. Lists can't determine it. When your identity is in the Rock—your identity is Rock Solid. As long as God is for you, it doesn't matter what mountain rises ahead of you. You aren't your yesterday, you aren't your messes, you aren't your lists. You are brave enough for today, because He is. You are strong enough for what's coming, because He is. And you are enough for all that is because He. always. is.
> —Ann Voskamp[31]

Hope has always been an important concept to me. Hope is like a tiny spark in the darkness that can kindle the flame to keep us warm. It's like a whisper of wind on the warmest day that leads to a pleasant breeze to cool our foreheads. I hear it when the birds sing in the dark, reminding us that the sun is going to rise. I see it when a tiny crocus pops up through the snow, telling us that spring will come again. I feel it when someone in the middle of so much pain says the word "but" as they remember God's love and tenderness.

When God told me the name of my ministry in the early days of putting it all together, I thought it was dumb. I've always

---
[31] Voskamp, Ann. "Only the Good Stuff: Multivitamins For Your Weekend." *Ann Voskamp*. November 12, 2022. https://annvoskamp.com/2022/11/only-the-good-stuff-multivitamins-for-your-weekend-11-12-2022/

loved hope, but it just seemed kind of stupid. Broken and Hopeful. What did that even mean? God has slowly unfolded His meaning in this name to me over the years. He tells me we don't have to be strong, whole, well, or fixed to have hope.

Hope isn't found in what we can achieve or fix, but in the person of Jesus and Who He is in us. So often we confuse positive thinking with hope. They are not the same thing. I love the way Henri Nouwen differentiates hope from optimism:

> HOPE ISN'T FOUND IN WHAT WE CAN ACHIEVE OR FIX BUT IN THE PERSON OF JESUS AND WHO HE IS IN US.

> *While optimism makes us live as if someday soon things will get better for us, hope frees us from the need to predict the future and allows us to live in the present, with deep trust that God will never leave us alone.*
> —Henri Nouwen[32]

Positive thinking, or optimism, promotes the idea that if we just keep telling ourselves things are better, or will get better, that will be true. Hope says that God is at work even in the pain, and He will never abandon us no matter how hard things get. We are not dependent on the outcome or the relief. Hope is a natural outflow of this relationship with God, as He reminds us He is not giving up on us, and He is making a way ahead. He is our Hope, so we can always have hope. Sometimes it is difficult to find this hope, though. How do we find hope in the present circumstance?

---

[32] Nouwen, Henri J. M. *The Dance of Life: Weaving Sorrows and Blessings Into One Joyful Step.* United Kingdom, Ave Maria Press, 2005. 210.

Breaking Free
Hope In Relationship

> *Now may God, the fountain of hope, fill you to overflowing with uncontainable joy and perfect peace as you trust in him. And may the power of the Holy Spirit continually surround your life with his superabundance until you radiate with hope!*
> —Romans 15:13

First, live in relationship abiding in the One who brings hope with Him. Focus deeply on the relationship with us for which God has fought, bled, and died to make possible, and for which He puts up with a lot of junk in us to maintain. He pursues us for relationship and puts us in the best place to know Him every day. We must simply lift our heads and look. He is our fountain of hope, and the Holy Spirit will enable you to radiate with hope.

Don't just live for the future. We don't have to wait for the sweet by-and-by for relationship with God. Eternal life is now! That is how He, Himself, defines eternal life. Some people end up being suicidal rapturists—wanting to be done with this life and obsessing over death or rapture as the way out. If the focus shifts to God and pushing into relationship with Him, freedom, relief, and peace come with Him! God's hope isn't just for the future, but for each day, each moment, right now. As we live in relationship with Him, we can see this hope.

> GOD'S HOPE ISN'T JUST FOR THE FURTURE BUT FOR EACH DAY, EACH MOMENT, RIGHT NOW.

Hannah Morrell

Set Your Mind

> Christ's resurrection is your resurrection too. This is why we are to yearn for all that is above, for that's where Christ sits enthroned at the place of all power, honor, and authority! Yes, feast on all the treasures of the heavenly realm and fill your thoughts with heavenly realities, and not with the distractions of the natural realm.
> Colossians 3:1–2

Set your mind on things above (Colossians 3:2). We get really distracted by the things around us and all the things we imagine or worry about. If I am focusing on all the junk, that junk will control me, which essentially amounts to worshipping that same junk. Ew! That's not what I want controlling my life! If I look away and focus on who God is in my situation and Who He is in me, my perspective shifts immediately. Eventually, the emotions follow the change in perspective (although they may take a little longer), but they must follow Truth. When I lead my emotions with Truth, I will feel better, too.

Stay in the present, not running to the future or the past. When we go to the past and live in regret, we poison the present and get sucked into obsession and guilt. Admit you are living there, repent, and leave the past at the feet of Jesus, taking forgiveness with you. Remember the divine janitor from Psalm 23 that we talked about in Chapter 2, following us around and cleaning up our messes? Leave the mess with your divine janitor, because if you try to clean it up, the only thing you will do is get covered in it.

I love the line in "Jireh" by Elevation Worship in which they sing, "I wasn't holding You up, so there's nothing I can do to let You down."[33] God loves us before our behavior lines up with the life we have. He is the One who eliminates our past, causing us not to be controlled by it anymore. You have no past. He has wiped it out and has freed us to live in the present with Him as we abide in Him.

The future is not a good place for us either. We worry and stress about how things will turn out or what we will do. If there is one thing I have learned from the stories in the Bible, it is that God will generally do things in the most backwards, upside-down-looking ways, ways that I never would have planned, so my planning doesn't do any good! When I leave the future in God's hands, He can make a way through all the impossible of life, doing it His way and for His glory. We can't help but look at Him in amazement and praise, as He works things out in His way. The beauty of abiding is that we stay in the present, connected as a branch to the Vine, and bearing fruit in a restful way. Nothing is a pressure or a stress to create as we set our minds on Christ enthroned in power, honor, and authority.

Don't Let Crazy People Tell You Who You Are

> Now, if anyone is enfolded into Christ, he has become an entirely new person. All that is related to the old order has vanished. Behold, everything is fresh and new.
> 2 Corinthians 5:17

One freedom God has been teaching me over the years has become a favorite for me: we are not to let crazy people tell us who we are. I would say that everyone is a little crazy, so it boils

---

[33] Elevation Worship and Maverick City Music. "Jireh." *Old Church Basement*. Charlotte, NC: Provident Label Group, 2021. Track 2.

down to not letting any human give you identity. We accept identity messages from people all the time, wearing names like "failure," "not good enough," "used," or "worthless" around unintentionally but as if agreeing with them. When we get off the roller coaster of other people's covert or overt communications to us, we can relax and not feel crazy ourselves. We identify the awful things that are now recorded in our head and spewed back by a tiny voice that I have heard someone call their "inner terrorist." When we see this for what it is, we call out the lies and interject Truth: God has given us a new identity, and the old one doesn't fit anymore. This is why we don't let crazy people tell us who we are. We can actually live as we are supposed to in the true identity God has given to us.

Only Jesus can tell us who we are, not parents, siblings, a spouse, or kids. Jesus says we are loved, accepted, worthy, holy, righteous, forgiven, and so much more! People constantly try to give us lies, mostly because they are fighting their own negative identity messages. We need to get better at saying "no, thank you" and moving back into the Truth as given by God and His Word. As we live according to what God says about us, we are free to see the truth and to live in rest, not running to a bunch of people to get acceptance. In relationship with Jesus, we recognize more and more who He is and who we are in Him as a new creation.

Breaking Free
Dealing With Problems

Are you weary, carrying a heavy burden? Come to me. I will refresh your life, for I am your oasis. Simply join your life with mine. Learn my ways and you'll discover that I'm gentle, humble, easy to please. You will find refreshment and rest in me.

Matthew 11:28–29

What do we do with problems? Don't ignore them; take them where they need to go—the feet of Jesus. I have talked previously in this book about how I love the story of Hezekiah when he gets awful news from an army general who has set his country as his next target and is going to destroy the entire population (2 Kings 19). Hezekiah takes the letter to the temple and spreads it out before the Lord, asking Him what to do. He doesn't come bringing plans, suggestions, expertise, or frankly, with a lot of hope. And God annihilates the army before they can even get to Hezekiah and his people. So often we need to just take our problems to God and lay them out before Him, waiting for His plan to deal with them.

We do feel emotions about these problems, but we pour those feelings out to God and stand on His promises. He loves us. He knows what is best to bring us to know Him every day. He is bringing forth His plan, which is for our good and to put us in the best place to know Him. It may not feel good, and His goal is not our comfort. But He loves our reliance on Him when we have circumstances that overwhelm us.

Discern the voice of the butcher versus the voice of the Shepherd. I have heard this contrast from several teachers, the first of whom was Mike Wells. The voice of the butcher

(Satan) is darkness, evil, shame, false guilt, regret, confusion, discouragement, depression, hopelessness, and failure. The voice of the Shepherd is life, light, hope, freedom, joy, peace, encouragement, and love. Determine whose voice you are listening to when you head downhill, understanding that you don't have to listen to the butcher. It doesn't do you any good to listen to him, and you can set your mind instead on the voice of the Shepherd Who loves you and keeps speaking truth to you.

Bob Goff says it this way:

If you hear a voice over your shoulder talking about your biggest failure and it isn't calling you 'beloved,' it isn't Jesus talking. Live undistracted.

—Bob Goff[34]

Another way to deal with problems is to focus on loving someone else. I find it interesting that the outcomes of several studies have shown exercise and helping others to be two of the best ways of dealing with depression. So often, we need to get our eyes off ourselves and invest in someone who needs help. We were created to love, even as our Father loves us (John 13:34). As we let Him be the source through us, we are no longer stunted and distorted by a complete focus on our own problems and how miserable we are. We can, instead, allow His love to flow out of us to others around us who need it.

Don't give up. Be entwined. Use the waiting to push more into entwining your heart with His. Waiting kind of stinks, but if

---

34 Goff, Bob [@bobgoff]. "If you hear a voice over your shoulder talking about your biggest failure and it isn't calling you 'beloved,' it isn't Jesus talking. Live undistracted." Twitter, May 18, 2022. https://twitter.com/bobgoff/status/1527034309130866688

you wring out every bit of pushing into the heart of Jesus, it will be worth it. When we don't get what we want on the timeline we want, we are often tempted to give up.

Dealing with Disappointments

Find your delight and true pleasure in Yahweh, and he will give you what you desire the most.
Psalm 37:4

Too often, I have heard people use this verse to justify giving up because God hasn't given them the desires of their hearts. I would suggest that maybe we don't even know the true desires of our hearts. We think they are things like a new car, a lot of money, a new (or first) spouse, or a thousand other things. But these gifts don't fix the problem and leave us wanting something else that we believe will satisfy. We go from one to the next, hoping that one desire will finally be enough to fulfill us. The items in the list above are blessings from God, and we will enjoy them. But the satisfaction isn't deep enough to really touch our hearts. We can thank Him when we get good things, but we can't place our worth or joy in them. They won't last, and we will end up disappointed. We were created for more!

Don't be distracted by desires that aren't big enough. We were created for a deep, passionate, loving relationship with God, Who knows us inside and out and delights in us. Spouses can have wonderful relationships with us, but they cannot touch the depth of a relationship with God. People will fail and disappoint us; they won't measure up. If we are trying to get life out of them, we will turn up empty. Only in relationship with this beautiful God can we be satisfied and truly live.

What Do We Get From Hope?

Here's what I've learned through it all: Don't give up; don't be impatient; be entwined as one with the Lord. Be brave and courageous, and never lose hope. Yes, keep on waiting—for he will never disappoint you!
Psalm 27:14

Hope in God gives us a faithful companion and deliverer who never betrays, never lies, and never abandons. He is with us through every single thing, never leaving us when it gets tough or being too upset by the choices we have made. He keeps asking us to come back to Him when we pull away, for we find our hope in Him.

Hope also gives us renewed strength and an ability to rise above any problem. When we recognize we are seated in the heavenlies with Jesus already (Ephesians 2:6), we can operate from that position. Things on the earth may look tough, but we have strength in Him beyond any we could generate personally. We do not have to stumble under anything that presents itself as too big.

Hope in God also gives us a good ending. I know we will end well because He is bringing us there. He is in charge of the beginning, middle, and ending (Philippians 1:6). Yes, we choose whether we walk with Him, but He's got the rest. So often, we think maintaining control is the only way we are going to end well, but we have to come to terms with the fact that we have very little control. Instead, we get to entrust Him with the whole shebang.

We also get resurrection life in every circumstance. Even the things which look dead are not dead to Him. When I first moved into my current house, I asked the former owner if she would walk me through the backyard and teach me how to care for it. The place was so beautiful, and I was terrified I was going to kill all of what she had so carefully planted and tended for many years. She was kind enough to give me a tour, but what she said increased my fear and trepidation. This lady told me to cut everything in the entire back yard down to the ground, and that was what would help it grow back to lush goodness.

Just before the onset of spring, I did as she had recommended, and when the deed was done, I told myself that this was probably the end of the beautiful backyard forever. To my great surprise, what looked like death was the beginning of amazing life and new growth. By July, my backyard was everything I wanted it to be, bursting with life and vigor. Nothing can limit God or what He can do to bring resurrection life to even the most dead-looking area (John 11:25–26).

Another wonderful gift we receive through hope in God is bridegroom love (1 Corinthians 13:7). He never lets us down, never gives up on us. He pursues us through hell and high water to find us and tell us that He loves us. So often, we look for this kind of love from a person when God has been loving us in this way all along. He is passionate, faithful, and perseverant.

We also get to enjoy freedom from fear (Isaiah 41:10). We don't need to be afraid of anything because God is going to carry us through, no matter what. This is a bold statement; I know. He is still dealing with fear in me, but He loves it out of me. When I believe I am loved, I also believe that the One Who loves me infinitely will support and carry me through, no matter what the pain, circumstance, or mess. Nothing can steal this relationship from me.

In addition to freedom from fear, we are freed from guilt. Guilt is a terrible motivator. It's not helpful or productive. I would differentiate between guilt and condemnation—condemnation is offered while guilt is receiving the condemnation and sitting in it. God says that condemnation is not ours to carry, and thus guilt is not either (Romans 8:1). When we hear the voice in our heads telling us we are guilty, remember Jesus took all of our guilt and sin to the cross. We negate His work of love on the cross when we try to take back our guilt or sin. They are not ours to carry, and it doesn't help us when we try to.

Better Than a Formula

Who could ever divorce us from the endless love of God's Anointed One? Absolutely no one! For nothing in the universe has the power to diminish his love toward us. Troubles, pressures, and problems are unable to come between us and heaven's love. What about persecutions, deprivations, dangers, and death threats? No, for they are all impotent to hinder omnipotent love, even though it is written: All day long we face death threats for your sake, God. We are considered to be nothing more than sheep to be slaughtered! Yet even in the midst of all these things, we triumph over them all, for God has made us to be more than conquerors, and his demonstrated love is our glorious victory over everything! So now I live with the confidence that there is nothing in the universe with the power to separate us from

Breaking Free

> *God's love. I'm convinced that his love will triumph over death, life's troubles, fallen angels, or dark rulers in the heavens. There is nothing in our present or future circumstances that can weaken his love. There is no power above us or beneath us—no power that could ever be found in the universe that can distance us from God's passionate love, which is lavished upon us through our Lord Jesus, the Anointed One!*
> Romans 8:35–39

There is no formula for hoping in God. It's a relationship. Often we want a formula with a guarantee to make us feel as if we have some control. We want the guarantee of a perfect marriage, joy, kids, financial stability. Instead, God promises us we will have tribulation—not the guarantee we would prefer. But that's not all. He also promises that He has overcome, and in Him, we are more than conquerors. That's an amazing guarantee and a pretty good feeling—to be more than a conqueror before we even see the battle. As we turn to Him for all we need, we can make it through anything, because He will carry us through.

My prayer for you as you reach the end of this book echoes Paul's prayer for the Ephesians:

> *I pray that the Father of glory, the God of our Lord Jesus Christ, would impart to you the riches of the Spirit of wisdom and the Spirit of revelation to know him through your deepening intimacy with him. I pray that the light of God will illuminate the eyes of your imagination, flooding you with light, until you experience the full revelation of the hope of his calling—that is, the wealth of God's glorious inheritances that he finds in us, his holy ones! I pray that you will continually experience the immeasurable greatness of God's power made available to you through faith. Then your lives will be an advertisement of this immense power as it works through you! This is the mighty power that was released when God raised Christ from the dead and exalted him to the place of highest honor and supreme authority in the heavenly realm!*
> Ephesians 1:17–20

With our hope in Jesus, we get to look past the giant, the fire, the lion's den, the angry people, the religious judgement, the criticism, the spouse, the health issue, the grief, the discouragement, the pressure, and the stress. We look past it all to the hope we have in Jesus right now. He lives with us, loves us infinitely, and is empowering us to handle each situation as it comes. Hope isn't just something we get in the future or after the future turns out the way we wanted it to. Hope is now. Relationship with Jesus is now. Resurrection life is now. Of course, it is also in the future, but don't wait to enjoy it! He is with us completely right now, loving us, desiring relationship with us, and carrying us deeper into His heart.

As we allow relationship with God to break us free from religion, we move into a life that is fun, joyful, and light. We have hope, even in times of suffering, because we recognize we are not trying to earn a place with God by our good behavior. We already are connected with God in relationship, but recognizing it brings relief and freedom. So often the Christian life seems impossible when we focus on trying to make God happy with lots of rules. But I would suggest that the Christian life is only possible as we abide in Christ, as He brings everything we need and produces fruit through us. Sink deeply into this connection in relationship to the God Who loves you immensely and find a way forward you never knew existed and couldn't imagine.

> HOPE IS NOW.
> RELATIONSHIP WITH JESUS IS NOW.
> RESURRECTION LIFE IS NOW.

Breaking Free
Going Deeper:

1. Look at each problem you face right now and ask Jesus to be enough for it and to draw you to a deeper entwining with Him through it.

2. Examine the messages you have received from "crazy people" and soak instead in the Truth He gives you.

3. Each day, wake up and tell Him you have no idea how you are going to do today. Then, thank Him for being enough for it.

4. Practice looking past whatever the presenting problem is to the One who holds you and the future, growing more comfortable in the position He has given you as a branch on the Vine.

Hannah Morrell

Recommended Reading

- *Sidetracked in the Wilderness*, by Michael Wells
- *Heavenly Discipleship*, by Michael Wells
- *The Scars That Have Shaped Me*, by Vaneetha Risner
- *Hardest Peace*, by Kara Tippetts
- *The Normal Christian Life*, by Watchmen Nee
- *The Reason for God*, by Tim Keller

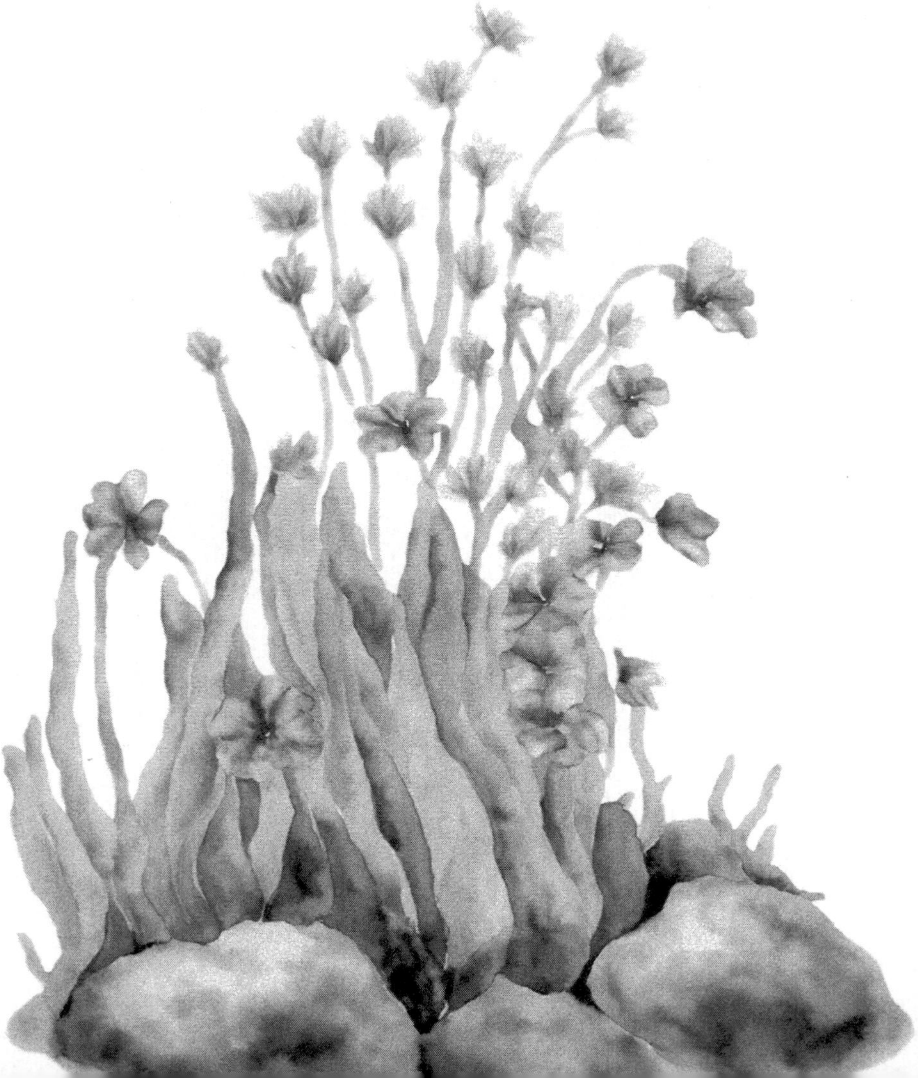

Made in the USA
Columbia, SC
03 December 2024